Developing Intuition

Developing Intuition

PRACTICAL GUIDANCE
FOR DAILY LIFE

SHAKTI GAWAIN

Nataraj Publishing

a division of

NEW WORLD LIBRARY
NOVATO, CALIFORNIA

Nataraj Publishing

a division of

New World Library
14 Pamaron Way
Novato, California 94949

Copyright © 2000 Shakti Gawain

Edited by Becky Benenate
Cover design by Alexandra Honig
Text design by Tona Pearce Myers

Library of Congress Cataloging-in-Publication Data
Gawain, Shakti, 1948–
Developing intuition : practical guidance for daily life /
Shakti Gawain.
p. cm.
Includes bibliographical references.
ISBN 1-57731-186-8(cloth : alk. paper)
1. Intuition (Psychology) 2. Intuition (Psychology)—
Problems, exercises, etc. I. Title.
BF315.5G39 2000
153.4'4—dc21

First paperback printing, February 2002
ISBN 1-57731-186-8
Printed in Canada on acid-free, partially recycled paper
Distributed to the trade by Publishers Group West

10 9 8 7 6 5 4 3 2 1

*This book is dedicated to all those
whose love and support
have made it possible
for me to do my work.*

CONTENTS

━ ACKNOWLEDGMENTS ━

I'd like to thank my editor Becky Benenate for her creative contributions, her emotional support, and all her hard work. This book would not have happened without you, Becky.

I appreciate all the ideas and contributions made by Marc Allen, Georgia Hughes, Lora O'Connor, Kathy Altman, and Gina Vucci. Thanks, too, to everyone at New World Library.

in•tu•ition — 1. the power or faculty of
attaining to direct knowledge or cognition
without evident rational thought
and inference.
2. quick and ready insight.

Why Develop Your Intuition?

Why commit your time and energy to the process of developing your intuition?

Quite simply because it's probably one of the most valuable things you will ever do for yourself. It actually takes relatively little time, and the potential rewards are enormous.

Intuition is an important resource that can greatly contribute to our success and fulfillment in life. It's a natural part of us — our <u>birthright</u> — and yet many of us have lost touch with it. Once we know how to follow it, intuition is a very accurate guiding force in all aspects of life. Without it, we are at a great disadvantage. It's a practical tool that we need in order to successfully deal with life.

Because our cultural values emphasize the

development of the rational, and scarcely acknowledge the existence or validity of intuition, many of us have lost touch with our intuitive sense. Fortunately, with a few simple exercises and a little practice, it is not difficult to reclaim. As you learn to follow your intuition, and it's validated by the results you get, you build self-trust and self-confidence.

In our modern complicated lives, where we often have so many choices and options, intuition can point us in the direction we need to go at any given moment. It can show us step by step what we need to do to fulfill our hearts' desires and achieve our goals. Our intuitive sense can help to keep us safe; it warns us when something may be harmful or dangerous.

Intuition always shows us the best route to where we need to go. Following it can save us a lot of confusion, hassle, and heartache.

As a friend of mine put it, "When I ignore my intuition I end up doing things that just don't work very well, or even things that aren't good for me. The more I follow my inner wisdom, the better I am able to care for myself, and the more things just fall into place."

Because intuition connects us to the soul level of our existence, many people who develop their intuition find that it brings them into a deep relationship with their spiritual nature, and brings that spiritual connection into their daily lives.

The most successful people are often very intuitive. Consciously or unconsciously, they follow their gut feelings. Intuition is closely connected to creativity; when we're out of touch with our intuitive sense we often find our creativity blocked. Following our intuition puts us "in the flow" — a very alive, productive, and desirable state.

If you are interested in getting more in touch with your intuition, read on.

INTRODUCTION

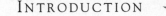

I was born into a family that was well educated and intellectual. My father was a professor of aeronautical engineering and my mother was a city planner. Both of my parents were highly rational people who greatly valued intellectual development.

I was a precocious child and an avid reader, and did well in school. I was praised and rewarded both at home and at school for my scholastic abilities and achievements.

I developed into an extremely logical person. I was quite skeptical, and prided myself on not believing anything that couldn't be scientifically proven. I considered myself an atheist and believed that God was an idea that people made up and clung to because they couldn't live with the fact that we don't really understand the meaning of our own existence.

In my college and early adult years, I began to have some experiences that didn't quite fit into my worldview. It was the 1960s, after all, and our entire culture was opening to a more holistic approach to life.

I became interested in eastern philosophies, and began to practice yoga and meditation. I studied modern dance in college, and found that sometimes when I was dancing I had an experience of feeling as if I was being "danced" by some force greater than myself. I attended some therapy groups where we shared deep feelings and, as a result, experienced transcendent feelings of closeness and oneness. All of these things began to open me to the nonlinear, nonrational aspect of my nature.

My mother was also exploring some of the same kinds of things. One day she called me excitedly and told me about a seminar she had just taken in which she had learned some techniques for intuitive development. She was quite amazed at the experiences she had had.

If it had been anyone other than my

mother, who I respected as a rational, intelligent person, my skeptical side would likely have brushed this off as a lot of nonsense. Instead, I was intrigued. Deep down inside of me, something that had long been buried began to stir. It was the feeling that there is a certain kind of magic in life, and that not everything can be explained in logical terms.

So I took the course that my mother recommended. I learned some meditation techniques, including the technique of visualization, where you imagine something that you want as if it were already true. I soon found this to be a very powerful tool that I subsequently used in my life on a regular basis.* I also learned how to access an inner guide, and a number of other useful skills. All of this was presented in a very clear, logical, almost scientific way that was appealing to my rational side.

At the end of the course, they had us do an exercise in which we would relax into a meditative state, and a facilitator would read from a card the name, age, and city of residence of a person none of us knew who had some type of ailment. (The name of the ailment was also

*I eventually wrote a bestselling book about it called *Creative Visualization*.

written on the card, but the facilitator didn't read that to us.) Then we would create a mental image of that person and notice what area of their body our attention was drawn to, and what feeling, thought or image we might get about that person's ailment. Many people had remarkable experiences of "guessing" one or more cases accurately.

My own experience was beyond remarkable — it was completely astounding. When my facilitator read the first person's name and information, I immediately had an image of the person in my mind. I started feeling my attention drawn to a certain area of her body, and I began to get a feeling of what her health problem might be. I said it aloud and it was correct. Since I "guessed" my first case correctly, they gave me another and another, and I guessed them accurately as well. I read ten cases in all and was correct with all of them.

This was a *shocking* experience for me. There was simply no logical way to explain what had happened. I had received the information in a different way than I was accustomed to getting information. It had not come through the usual routes of my five senses. I felt as if my mind had dropped into a kind of groove or channel and the information was just there.

That experience opened me up to the fact that we have another way of accessing information and knowledge, through our intuitive faculty. After that I was fascinated to learn more about how I could connect with that part of myself. I suspected that it could be a very powerful and practical help to me in my life if I could learn how to use it that way. I began to practice some of the simple techniques I had learned in the course, and found them very helpful.

Not long after that I went on an extended two year journey. It began with a vacation in Italy and developed into a year of traveling and working in Europe, followed by going overland to India, spending several months traveling around India, and eventually going all the way around the world.

This entire journey was a marvelous experience of learning to follow my intuition. Although I wasn't completely aware of it at the time, in retrospect I was certainly being prompted by some inner guidance every step along the way. I had no definite plans, and usually didn't know where I was going to eat or sleep that night. I just took one day at a time and allowed things to unfold, which they did in a rather remarkable way. I had almost no possessions and very little money, yet somehow I was always taken care of. I encountered many difficult and challenging situations, yet everything worked out. It was a great experience in learning to trust myself and follow the flow of life.

When I returned home I was very interested in pursuing my personal development and learning more about how I could balance and integrate rationality and intuition in my life.

In the years following I was blessed with a number of teachers who helped me learn to trust my intuition and use it as a guiding force in my life. The practice of listening to and following my inner guidance became a very important part of my life, and still is. I've discovered that using your intuition on a daily basis is one of the most important keys to self-development.

In this book I hope to pass on to you what I have learned, in simple, practical ways that will enhance the quality of your life, and help you fulfill your dreams.

CHAPTER ONE

What Is Intuition?

There is a universal, intelligent life force that exists within everyone and everything. It resides within each one of us as a deep wisdom, an inner knowing. We can access this wonderful source of knowledge and wisdom through our intuition, an inner sense that tells us what feels right and true for us at any given moment.

Many people who are not accustomed to being consciously in touch with their intuition imagine that it is a mysterious force that would come to them through some transcendent mystical experience. In fact, our intuition is a very practical, down-to-earth tool that is always available to help us deal with the decisions, problems, and challenges of our daily lives. One way that we often describe an intuitive prompting is as a "gut feeling" or a "hunch."

Intuition is a natural thing. We are all born with it. Young children are very intuitive, although in our culture they are often trained out of it early in life.

We are accustomed to thinking that some people are intuitive and some aren't. Women are generally considered to be more intuitive than men, for example. Yet many men follow their hunches on a regular basis. In reality, we are all potentially intuitive. Some of us consciously develop this ability, while a majority of us learn to disregard and deny it. Still, many people are unconsciously following their intuition without realizing it.

Fortunately, with some practice most of us can reclaim and develop our natural intuitive abilities. We can learn to be in touch with our intuition, to follow it, and to allow it to become a powerful guide in our lives.

In many cultures, including those of most of the indigenous peoples of the world, intuition is acknowledged, respected, and honored as a natural and important aspect of life. Every moment of daily life is guided by a strong sense of connection to the universal creative force. These societies create powerful rituals, such as group councils, dream sharing, chants, dances, and vision quests, that support their connection to the inner intuitive realms. Individuals within those cultures learn to trust and follow their own inner sense of truth and offer it as their wisdom to others. They have a profound sense of the interconnectedness of all life.

Our modern western culture, on the other hand, does not acknowledge the validity or even the existence of intuition. We respect, honor, and develop the rational aspect of our nature and, at least until recently, have disregarded and discounted the intuitive side.

Our school system reflects and reinforces this bias. It focuses almost exclusively on developing our left-brain, rational abilities and mostly ignores the development of the right-brain, intuitive, holistic, creative capacities. We often see the same bias in the business world. Only in recent years have some schools and businesses begun to truly value intuition, and to encourage the kind of creativity and progressive thinking that results from intuitive awareness.

The rational mind is like a computer — it processes the input it receives and calculates logical conclusions based on this information. The rational mind is finite; it can only compute the data that it has received directly from the external world. In other words, our rational minds can only operate on the basis of the direct experience each of us has had in this lifetime — the knowledge we have gained through our five senses.

The intuitive mind, on the other hand, seems to have access to an infinite supply of information, including information that we have not gathered directly through personal experience. It appears to be able to tap into a deep storehouse of knowledge and wisdom — the *universal mind*. It is also able to sort out this information and supply us with exactly what we need, when we need it. Although the message may come through a bit at a time, if we learn to follow this flow of information step by step, the necessary course of action will be revealed. As we learn to rely on this guidance, life takes on a flowing, effortless quality. Our life, feelings, and actions interweave harmoniously with those of others around us.

In suggesting that our intuition needs to be the guiding force in our lives, I am not attempting to disregard or eliminate the intellect. Our rational faculty is a very powerful tool that can help us organize, understand, and learn from our experiences, so of course it is important to educate our minds and develop our intellectual capacities. However, if we attempt to direct our life primarily from our intellect, we are likely to miss out on a great deal. In my experience, it works best to balance and integrate logic with intuition.

Many of us have programmed our intellect to doubt our intuition. When an intuitive feeling arises, our rational minds immediately say, "I don't think that will work," or "What a foolish idea," and the intuition is disregarded. We must train our intellect to respect, listen to, and express the intuitive voice.

Most of us have spent a lifetime developing our rational minds. Fortunately it doesn't take a long time or a lot of work to develop our intuitive abilities. In fact, I've facilitated thousands of people in this process and I've found that with a little explanation and practice the vast majority of them are able to get in touch with their intuition and begin following it on a regular basis. From there, the whole process of balancing logic with intuition happens easily and naturally.

Intuition and Instinct

People often use the term instinct inter-changeably with intuition. In reality, instinct and intuition are different, but related.

Animals live by their instinct, a genetically programmed part of them that naturally directs them toward survival and reproduction. Human beings are animals and we also have instinctual energies that prompt us toward self-preservation and the preservation of our species. In addition to instinct, we humans have intuition, a faculty which gives us a much broader spectrum of infor-mation, related not only to our survival but our growth, development, self-expression, and higher purpose. Instinctual behavior is usually similar in all members of a given species, whereas intuition seems to be fine-tuned to our individual needs in any given moment.

As human beings have become more "civi-lized," we have tended to repress and disown our instinctual energies, such as aggression and sex-uality. To some extent that may be necessary to have an orderly, law-abiding society. If our instincts become overly repressed, however, we lose a lot of our life energy, and our natural capacity to take care of ourselves. When we

26

disown our instinctual energies we often lose touch with our intuition as well. So we need to develop a healthy balance of intellect, instinct, and intuition. (We will discuss more about developing and balancing the different energies within us in chapter 8.)

Intuition and Psychic Ability

When people begin learning about intuition, one question that often comes up is, "What is the difference, if any, between intuition and psychic ability?"

The word *psychic* can be frightening for many people. They may associate the term with weird, far-out phenomena. Some may have had a confusing or disturbing psychic experience themselves or know someone who has. They may have read about or encountered psychics who are strange, flamboyant, inaccurate, or untrustworthy. Some people have simply seen too many Hollywood movies in which psychic abilities are presented in a dark and frightening way.

The terms *intuitive* and *psychic* are often used more or less synonymously. If intuition is equated with psychic ability, some may fear that developing their intuition will lead them

27

somewhere they don't want to go. Others feel the opposite: They are fascinated with the idea of being psychic and for various reasons want to develop that ability.

I would like to clarify my understanding and use of the two terms. As I have said, intuition is a natural ability that we are all born with. If our family and our culture support our intuitive gift, it will develop into a natural and practical asset. If not, it may go undeveloped unless and until we choose to consciously focus on developing it. Some people, however, have an especially strongly developed intuitive sense. They may be born with it, or they may develop it early in life. These are the people we think of as natural psychics. Others may consciously *choose* to develop their intuitive abilities to the point where they become psychic.

People who are psychic may receive a great deal of intuitive information about themselves and others. Like any other talent, this can be a mixed blessing. Their challenge is to learn to manage this ability in such a way that it works in their lives.

So we are really talking about a spectrum of experience.

UNDEVELOPED —— DEVELOPED —— PSYCHIC
INTUITION   INTUITION   ABILITY

On one end of the spectrum, we have not developed our intuitive gifts. As we move to the center we are learning to follow the daily, moment-to-moment intuitive feelings that nudge us in the direction we need to go. They are not usually very dramatic and they generally give us only the information we need at that moment. If we move farther along the spectrum we may have more frequent and perhaps more dramatic experiences in which we have a strong feeling, a clear vision, or receive a lot of information. There is an infinite range of experiences on this spectrum, and we may fluctuate at different times to different places on the spectrum. For example, sometimes a person with a totally undeveloped intuition has a spontaneous dramatic psychic experience.

This book is focused primarily on helping you explore and find your balance in the middle ground of the spectrum. It's about accessing and learning to trust your natural intuitive ability so that it can take its rightful place as a positive guiding force in your life. Wherever you currently are on the spectrum, it can help you get comfortable with your intuition in a simple, practical way that really works in your life.

RECALLING AN INTUITIVE FEELING EXERCISE

Throughout this book there will be a number of exercises and meditations to help you develop your intuition. Some of you may wish to keep a journal or notebook to write about your experiences and insights.

Get in a comfortable position, close your eyes and take a few slow, deep breaths.

See if you can remember a time when you had a strong hunch, a gut feeling, or a feeling of "knowingness" about something. How did it come to you? How did it feel?

Did you follow it? What happened as a result of following it or not following it?

If you want to, write a little bit in your journal or a notebook about this experience.

If you didn't remember ever having a hunch, gut feeling, or feeling of knowingness, that's perfectly okay and normal. Many people are not in touch with their intuition in this way yet. Read on....

CHAPTER TWO

Becoming Aware

*A*ll of us have intuitive feelings all the time. Many of us, however, automatically ignore, discount, or contradict those feelings. Usually this is an unconscious process; we aren't even aware that we've had an intuitive prompting and discarded it. We brush it aside so quickly we don't even realize that it's happened, and that some deeper part of us may be trying to get our attention.

For example, when presented with an opportunity, you might get an instant deep feeling and think, for a moment, "Wow, I'd love to do this!" or "This really feels right for me." Immediately after that you may think, "Well, I can't do that. That's silly!" or "What would my family think" or "Gee, I really don't know anything about that. I might fail or make a real fool out of myself." Then you may push the whole idea aside without considering it further.

A friend of mine told me that her husband had brought home a man he was thinking about hiring as a partner at his firm. She found him to be perfectly pleasant, but felt for some reason he would not be a good partner for the firm. She couldn't really put her finger on why, so she dismissed how she felt, didn't say anything to her husband, and the person was hired. Within a few days her husband told her that they were having difficulties with their new partner, and that the firm would have to let him go and start the whole recruiting process all over again.

Although my friend dismissed her intuitive feelings at the time, her intuition was validated several days later. I've seen this happen countless times in my own life and in the lives of those around me. You've probably seen it happen, too.

Developing your intuitive ability begins with paying attention to what's going on inside of you so that you can become aware of these inner dialogues and catch them when they are happening, or shortly afterward. As you become more aware of your inner process, you will begin to notice the intuitive feelings as they pop up, and you will then be able to deal with them more consciously.

Most people find that with a little practice and time, they become much more aware of their intuitive feelings. The next challenge is to learn how to interpret them and act on them in a practical way. The information and exercises in this book will help you to develop all of these skills.

33

Remember that feeling and following your intuition is a completely natural process. You were born with this ability and you had it as a young child. To whatever degree you've forgotten or lost touch with this skill, with a little practice you can reclaim it.

Here are a few examples of different ways that people experience intuitive feelings:

A friend of mine once shared with me that whenever her phone rings, she knows, nine times out of ten, who's calling before she answers. When she first noticed this happening she thought it was a little strange. Now she gets a kick out of it and even makes it a game with herself. Have you ever felt like you knew who was calling before answering the phone? Or, how many times have you been thinking about someone and the phone rings and it's the person you were thinking about?

I've often had the experience of thinking of a certain song that I haven't heard in months or years, and then hearing it on the radio a short time later. My editor says that she often senses that there is something important in the mail several days before she receives the package. Have you ever felt something important was "coming," but were unable to put your finger on what that "something" was?

34

Many people tune into their intuition while participating in sports, while at work, or at school. Have you ever felt that you *knew* the teacher was going to call on you, and she did? Or, you *knew* that you were going to hit a home run or sink a putt, and did?

Most successful people follow their gut feelings when making business and investment decisions. Research scientists often follow a hunch about which line of experimentation will be most fruitful. Einstein was a wonderful example of a scientist who was clearly in touch with his intuition. The famous story of Edison dreaming of the light bulb is a beautiful example of how intuition interweaves with science, and how intuitive guidance can come through our dreams.

The vast majority of our intuitive feelings, however, are so ordinary and mundane that we might not even think of them as intuition. Suppose, for example, you're at a pleasant social gathering and you realize that, for no particular reason, you are feeling like you need to leave. Another voice inside of you may jump in immediately and say, "That's silly. You can't leave! What will people think?" So you may stay in a situation where you really don't want to be. If you do trust your intuitive feeling and act on it, you may find that you just needed some alone time. Or something unexpected and special might happen on the way home, or you might get home just in time to get an important phone call. When we follow our intuition we often don't know exactly what we are doing or why, but there are usually some surprising and interesting results.

Awareness Exercise

If you sense that you may have intuitive feelings that you are in the habit of ignoring or disregarding, try this exercise every evening for a week or so.

Sit or lie down in a comfortable position where you won't be disturbed. A warm bath can be a nice place to do this, but any quiet place is fine. Take a few slow, deep breaths and allow your body and mind to relax.

Now think back to when you first woke up this morning. How were you feeling? What were you thinking about? What did you do after you woke up? Now slowly review your day, remembering anything of significance that happened and how you felt about it. Try not to get caught up in it right now; just review it as if you were watching a movie of your day.

As you are doing this, try to notice specifically if there was any time during the day when you might have had an intuitive feeling about something — an impulse to do something different than usual, a hunch of some kind, a feeling of rightness or wrongness about something, a feeling of knowing something without knowing why, a feeling of a lot of energy, enthusiasm, or "juice" for a possible action, or conversely, a feeling of deadness or lack of energy in relation to a possible action.

If you become aware of a time during the day when you may have had a feeling like this, try to remember how you handled it. Did you pay attention to that feeling and explore it? Or did you quickly discount it and push it aside? How did you feel afterward?

In general, when we follow a true intuitive feeling, things tend to work out well (although sometimes in very unexpected and surprising ways), we feel energized and enlivened, and there's a sense of being "in the flow" of life. When we don't follow our intuition, we often feel somewhat depleted, depressed, or numb, and there may be a sense of being blocked, having to push to make things happen, or being "out of the flow."

At this point, it may be difficult to distinguish your intuitive feelings from many other kinds of inner voices and feelings. We will work with learning to distinguish intuition from other feelings later in the book. For now, just do your best to notice whether you *might* have had an intuitive feeling and if so how you handled it.

If you're not sure whether you ever have intuitive feelings, don't worry. Just keep reading and working with the exercises and very likely more clarity will come.

Once you have finished reviewing your day, noticing how you handled any possible intuitive feelings you may have had, it's time to let it all go and just relax. Remember, this is an experience in *awareness*. The purpose is to help you become more conscious of your relationship to your intuition, so that you can learn to develop that relationship. So please do not judge or criticize yourself in any way if you notice that you are not in the habit of paying attention to your intuitive feelings. In fact, this would be an excellent time to appreciate yourself for your desire and willingness to learn and grow!

If you are keeping a journal, you may wish to write a little about what you learn or experience each evening when you do this exercise.

Some of you may find that this practice of reviewing your day and learning from it is so helpful that you wish to continue it as a regular awareness practice.

38

CHAPTER THREE

Trusting Yourself

One of the reasons that many of us do not learn to trust and follow our intuition is that we are taught from an early age to try to accommodate those around us, to follow certain rules of behavior, to suppress our spontaneous impulses, and to do what is expected of us. We also learn to look to outside authorities for answers and direction rather than looking or listening within ourselves.

Those outside authorities can take many different forms. As children, our authorities may be our parents, grandparents, or older siblings, our religion (which may invoke God as the ultimate authority figure!), our schools and teachers, our peer group, and our community values and mores. Later on as adults we may also look to our spouses, employers, doctors, lawyers, and other experts of various kinds.

Of course, as children it is necessary and appropriate for us to receive guidance and direction from our parents, teachers, and others who have the responsibility to help us grow and develop. Even as adults we often need information and opinions from others who know more than we do about something.

The problem is that we learn to look to the outside authority instead of paying attention to our own feelings and intuitive promptings. We come to believe that life's answers lie somewhere outside of us, and we develop a lifelong habit of looking to others. We think that somebody else knows better than we do about what's true for us. We learn not to trust ourselves and our own sense of truth, our own inner authority.

A woman in one of my workshops owned and managed a successful public relations business. She told me she had always been awed by businesswomen she met who had MBAs, because she did not have a formal business education. At one point she hired a woman with an

MBA as a consultant. This woman advised her to make some changes that intuitively did not feel right to her. She trusted the consultant's expertise more than her own sense of things, however, and followed the advice — with some unfortunate consequences. She told me she had really learned her lesson from this and subsequently always trusted her own gut feelings in making decisions about her business.

I know a woman whose daughter had always been a straight-A student. Suddenly her grades started to plummet. The woman tried to talk with her about what was happening but she wouldn't say much. The woman shared her concerns with many of her close friends and family. All of them told her not to worry, it was a phase and it would pass. She eventually took her daughter to see a therapist and the therapist also told her that her daughter was exhibiting "typical teenage" behavior — and not to be too concerned. The woman's intuition kept telling her something very serious and dangerous was happening to her daughter, and because of this "feeling" she kept looking for clues to what was happening.

Eventually she found evidence that her daughter was regularly using drugs. When confronted about it her daughter broke down and confided in her that she "couldn't get ahold of herself, and needed help." She removed her daughter from the influences she was involved in and got her into a therapeutic/rehab school. A year and a half later, her daughter is doing much better, and is far along the road to recovery. She is working through her depression and has been drug free for two years. For the first time in her daughter's life, she likes who she is. The mother and daughter have become very close, they both feel they have survived, and the daughter is grateful that her mother didn't give up.

This story shows us that, even though family, friends, and outside professionals continued to tell the woman "nothing was wrong," she *knew* her daughter was in danger and wouldn't dismiss her intuition.

Unfortunately, the pattern of giving too much power to "outside authorities" leads some of us who are seeking personal development or spiritual growth to become overly dependent upon a teacher or guru to give us answers and show us our path. Equally unfortunately, there are many teachers in the personal growth movement who consciously or unconsciously encourage this type of dependency because they enjoy being in the position of power and it can be quite lucrative, or because they sincerely believe that they are helping people this way. This type of relationship with a teacher can sometimes be positive at a certain stage in a person's learning process. Sooner or later, however, we must recognize that deep down, the only one who knows what's true and right for us is our own innate wisdom. We must learn to trust our own "inner teacher," which comes to us through our intuitive guidance.

Once we learn the habit of listening to our intuition and trusting our inner responses, we can develop a very different kind of relationship with teachers, doctors, or any other kind of expert. If we need support or knowledge, we can follow our gut feelings about who to go to for help or advice. We can listen with respect and an open mind to what that person has to say, trusting that if we were drawn to them, there is likely to be value there for us. Then we can ponder what they have told us, paying attention to our intuitive feelings about what is right for us and what isn't, and making our own decisions about what course of action to follow. In other words, we are open to learning and receiving guidance from others as needed, while not giving our power and authority away to anyone else.

For example, a friend of mine was having a painful back problem. The doctor he consulted advised him that surgery would be necessary. He scheduled the surgery, but began to realize that he was feeling very uncertain whether this was the right step. He had an intuitive feeling to consult another doctor for a second opinion. This doctor suggested that he postpone the surgery for a while and work with an osteopath and a massage therapist. As it turned out, in a few months time, his back was healed without surgery.

44

I'm not implying that one should disregard a doctor's advice, or that surgery isn't the most appropriate treatment in many situations. This is simply a good example of someone paying attention to his intuitive hunch, and seeking other alternatives before making an important decision.

It's not only the habit of looking to outside authority figures that can cause us to doubt or discount our own intuitive feelings. Often times the ways we relate with our families and friends make it difficult to hear or trust our own intuitive voice. Many of us have the pattern of being overly concerned with pleasing or caretaking our loved ones, or trying to live up to their expectations of us. We may have difficulty even acknowledging our intuitive feelings if we fear that following them could upset or disappoint someone we care about.

A client of mine was having difficulty admitting to himself that he needed some alone time. He felt guilty about not spending all of his free time with his wife and children. Eventually he acknowledged his feelings, first to himself and then to his family. As it turned out, it was not so difficult to work out a solution where he took one evening a week entirely for himself.

Obviously in all relationships, compromise and negotiations have to be made. It's surprising, though, how often things work themselves out when everyone concerned can express their needs and feelings, including their intuitive feelings.

A close friend of mine recently told me that shortly before her first marriage, she and her fiancé had a long, honest talk and realized that the marriage felt like a mistake for both of them. They simply could not bring themselves to disappoint and upset their families and friends, however, so they went ahead with the wedding, and remained married for several unhappy

45

years. It would have taken an enormous act of courage to support their truth and call off the wedding, but it could have saved years of pain and struggle. In reality, they probably had intuitive feelings that the marriage was wrong long before they talked about it, when it would have been easier to take appropriate action.

LEARNING TO TRUST EXERCISE

Get in a comfortable position, close your eyes and take a few slow, deep breaths. Can you remember a time when you had an intuitive feeling about something, but disregarded it and went along with someone else's feeling or opinion? How did you feel afterward? How did things work out?

Write a bit about this experience, if you wish.

CHAPTER FOUR

Learning to Relax

One of the keys to getting in touch with your intuition is learning to relax your mind and relax your body sufficiently so that you can allow your attention to move out of your head and literally "drop down" into a deeper place in your body, closer to where your gut feelings reside. Simply letting your awareness move into a deeper place in your body in this way is tremendously helpful in opening the door to intuition.

In the modern world, we are so accustomed to living in a state of stress that many of us don't really know how to relax physically, mentally, and emotionally except when we're sleeping — and some of us not even then!

In order to get the most benefit from the

exercises in this book, it's important to be able to relax your body and your mind. Each meditation begins with a brief relaxation practice that will be effective for many of you. Some of you may already have a favorite relaxation or meditation technique that works well for you. If so, feel free to use it as a preparation for the meditations in this book.

If you would like more practice in relaxation, try the following exercise, which will probably leave you feeling calm and peaceful.

RELAXATION EXERCISE

This exercise is designed for very deep relaxation. Just as with learning any kind of new activity, such as riding a bicycle or running, it takes a while to train your body and mind to respond in a new way. The instructions given here will help you achieve a balanced and effective relaxation response in a minimum of time. Once you have done this longer version a few times, you'll discover that you can enter a deeply relaxed state within just a few seconds by closing your eyes and taking a few deep breaths.

First give yourself permission to take five to ten minutes to relax deeply, without having to think about other things you should be doing. Choose a quiet place and time of day when this will be possible. Loosen any tight clothing.*

Sit in an alert, upright position in a comfortable chair with your lower back well supported, hands gently resting in your lap with your palms open. Or, lie down on your back with a small pillow under your neck and a pillow under your knees if needed for comfort.

Take a deep breath and exhale slowly, allowing your shoulders to be loose and relaxed.

Open your mouth wide. Yawn, or pretend you are yawning.

Let the areas around your eyes and forehead be relaxed and loose. Let the areas around your nose, mouth, and jaw be relaxed.

Breathe slowly and easily.

If ideas or feelings come into your mind at this time, pretend they are a telephone ringing in the distance, perhaps in a neighbor's house. You acknowledge that "someone is calling" but you do not have to answer.

Take a deep breath, inhaling gently and slowly, imagining the breath entering your right

49

*This exercise was contributed by Hal Bennett and also appears in my book, *The Path of Transformation*.

nostril. Hold the breath for a moment, then exhale slowly and comfortably, imagining that you are exhaling through your left nostril.

Take another deep breath, this time imagining your breath entering your left nostril and exiting your right.

Focus your attention on how your breath feels: cooling, as it enters your nostrils, perhaps gently expanding your chest as it fills your lungs, then slightly warming your nostrils as you exhale. You may wish to visualize the air as having a beautiful, vibrant color as it enters and exits your body.

Repeat this breathing pattern until you have done at least four full cycles. A full cycle is one inhalation and one exhalation through each nostril.

With each cycle, focus your attention on one area of your body:

Be aware of your feet relaxing.

Be aware of your legs relaxing.

Be aware of your buttocks relaxing.

Be aware of your abdomen relaxing.

Be aware of your arms and hands relaxing.

Be aware of your upper back relaxing.

Be aware of your chest relaxing.

Be aware of your neck and shoulders relaxing.

Be aware of your head relaxing.

Now let your breathing pattern return to normal as you enjoy the relaxed state you have created.

Practice this relaxation exercise whenever the opportunity arises or whenever you feel a need to unwind and rest at work, at home, or in your recreational life. Also, if you like, practice it before doing any of the meditations in this book.

If you have real difficulty relaxing and this exercise doesn't help you, I have some other suggestions:

1. Do something enjoyable that requires physical exertion — walking, running, or playing lively music and dancing — until you feel tired. Then lie down and relax deeply.

2. Play quiet relaxing music that you love while you lie down and let the music wash through you.

3. Listen to a guided meditation tape.

4. Take a meditation, yoga, or stress reduction class.

With practice, bringing yourself to a relaxed state will become almost effortless. You will most likely be able to deeply relax with just a few deep breaths. Like developing any new skill, you may have difficulty at first; as you practice, however, it will become easier.

Be kind to yourself. Don't push yourself or you may find the exercise more stressful than relaxing. Remember that you are preparing yourself to listen to what you already know.

CHAPTER FIVE

Accessing Intuition

Many of us are aware of spontaneously having intuitive "flashes" from time to time. As you read this book, you may become aware that you have intuitive feelings more often than you realized, and that you have discounted many of them without knowing it.

The truth is, our intuitive wisdom is always there inside of us and it is always trying to come through to guide us. Most of us simply don't know how to access it at will on a regular basis. Fortunately we can learn to do exactly that.

Here is a basic meditation for getting in touch with your intuitive guidance. I have used this meditation myself for about twenty years, and have taught thousands of people to access their intuition through this practice.

Inner Guidance Meditation

Find a quiet, peaceful place where you will be undisturbed for a few minutes. Sit or lie down in a comfortable position with your spine straight and well supported. Close your eyes.

Take a deep breath, and as you exhale slowly, relax your body. Take another deep breath and as you exhale, relax your body a little more. Take another deep breath and as you exhale, relax your body as deeply and completely as you can. If any place in your body feels tight or tense, gently breathe into that area and allow it to release and relax.

Now take another deep breath and as you exhale, relax your mind. Let your thoughts just drift away. As each new thought comes up in your mind, let it go. There is no need to hold onto any thought. Just keep letting them go and bringing your attention back to breathing slowly and deeply and relaxing.

Take another deep breath and as you exhale, imagine that you can move your awareness out

54

of your mind, out of your head, and drop it slowly down into your body. Let it rest in the area of your solar plexus or your belly.

Now take another deep breath, and as you exhale, let your awareness move into a very deep quiet place within. With every breath as you exhale, move a little deeper and a little deeper until you come to rest in the deepest, quietest place you can find. Then just let yourself rest in this quiet place inside.

In this quiet place inside, you naturally have access to your intuitive inner guidance. You could think of it as a wise part of you that lives in this deep place within you. It knows exactly what you need at every moment.

55

Ask yourself in this deep place, "What do I most need to remember or be aware of right now?"

After you ask this question, just rest quietly and be open to what might come. Notice if a thought, a feeling, or an image comes to you in response to this question. Just take whatever comes and be with it for a little while. It's not necessary to understand it. Just be with it in a receptive way.

You may feel like you are "making something up." If so, that's okay — and it's always interesting to note what you have chosen to "make up" at that moment. Just allow whatever is happening to happen.

You may feel that nothing is happening, or that you get nothing. That's okay too. Don't try to make something happen. Trying gets in the way of the process. If nothing is coming right now, just accept that.

If you *have* received some thought, feeling, and/or image, allow yourself to sit with it a little bit. When you feel complete with the process for now, begin to notice your breath again. Notice how your body is feeling and become aware of your surroundings. When you are ready, you can open your eyes.

If you wish, you can write down whatever you experienced or whatever "message" you received. Otherwise, just contemplate your experience a bit before you go about any other activities.

This is an excellent exercise to do in the morning before you start your day, or at night before you go to sleep. If possible, do it at least once a day for a while; twice a day is even better. If you can't manage that, try for once or twice a week. Once you get used to it, you can easily do this exercise in five to ten minutes.

56

In this meditation I used a very general question "What do I most need to remember or be aware of right now?" I have found that this question works well for many people to open to whatever their intuition may wish to communicate. You can use any question that works for you, however, including more specific ones such as, "What direction do I need to go right now?" or "Show me my next step," or "How do I need to take care of myself?" or even "Should I take the job I've been offered?"

After you have done this meditation, pause occasionally throughout the day and notice what's going on inside of you. Over the next few days, try to be aware of any thoughts, feelings, and experiences related to the question you have asked. Practice following any intuitive impulses you have, and notice how things work out.

People have different kinds of experiences with this exercise. Many people find that a thought, feeling, and/or image comes to them during the meditation that is clearly relevant and immediately helpful. The more you practice this exercise, the more likely it is that you will receive clear, simple messages that you can easily interpret and understand.

As I mentioned, some people get a response but feel like they are "making it up" rather than experiencing it as "coming to them." My feeling is that it's best to trust whatever is happening, as long as it basically feels right to you. Worrying about whether you are doing it right blocks the process; trusting your own experience opens up the process. So if you feel like you are making something up, just go ahead and do it. Chances are that whatever you "make up" will be relevant.

I recently did this exercise with a group and here are a few examples of "messages" that came to the participants:

One woman received the message "Have more fun!"

She saw an image of riding on a carousel followed by an image of swimming in the warm ocean in Mexico at night.

These are both fun, physically enjoyable, sensuous experiences not involving the mind. This woman is a very mental person. She felt that her intuition was showing her that she needs to enjoy her physical body more.

One woman saw a sign in big letters saying HEALTH.

She was dealing with some health issues and interpreted this as a reminder to focus her attention on her health.

A man had an image of sitting on a warm beach by the ocean. The feeling was "Everything is okay."

Another woman heard the words "Trust, not fear."
She interpreted this as a message not to worry, to relax and trust her own process.

A woman had an image of a large brown bear with quiet strength, so powerful that he doesn't need to be aggressive.
This is a frequent image for this woman, representing her personal power that she's learning to own. This time the bear was excited and happy, almost dancing, because the woman has had a recent breakthrough where she was able to stay with her own power in a difficult situation.

For one man these words came: "Love is the answer."
This man had recently had a very upsetting experience and was feeling very angry. He felt this

59

*was a reminder not to polarize too far into anger
and remember the power of forgiveness.*

One man had an image of himself in a
meadow with a powerful woman he respects.
She was on a horse and dressed in a warrior/god-
dess costume. He was bowing reverentially to
her. She said to him, "Don't give your power
away. Don't be so adoring! You are my knight!"

*He felt this related to a pattern he has of giving
his own power away to women. The woman in the
image represented his powerful inner feminine
side.*

60

One woman, who is usually very visual, just
had a peaceful feeling inside.

Some people receive a message that is
unclear or difficult to understand or interpret.
Don't worry about trying to understand it logically. Like our dreams, the images or feelings
that come to us are often working on a level
below the conscious mind. Don't obsess about
the meaning of it. Let it go and assume that it's
working on a deeper level. Sometimes the
meaning will come clear later, in some spontaneous way.

For example, a participant in one of my workshops got an image of a bright red-hot burning fire one day during this meditation. She had no idea what it meant. A couple of days later she woke with the realization that she was carrying a lot of anger that she needed to express and work with. Her intuition was letting her know the next step in her healing process. Of course, the same image might have a totally different meaning for someone else.

Even if you never get a conscious understanding of an intuitive message, don't be concerned. If it's important, it will come to you again, one way or another.

If you feel that you didn't get any type of feeling, thought, or image in response to your question during the meditation, that's not a cause for concern either. Here are two possible reasons:

1. If you are new to all this, or this is the first time you've tried this exercise, it may take a little time and practice before you feel relaxed and open enough to trust your experience.

2. Even for the most experienced and highly intuitively developed people, the message we need to hear often does not come at the

moment that we ask. There is often a "delayed response." We ask inside for some type of intuitive guidance and we get nothing in the moment. However, a few hours or a few days later, we may get a spontaneous awareness, thought, or feeling, that is really the answer to the question we had asked.

Another very interesting thing is that our intuition may respond to our request internally, in all the ways I have been describing, but we are just as likely to receive a response from what seems like an external source.

62

For example, you may ask for an intuitive message in your meditation one morning, but not receive any information. That evening as you walk home from work you may have the impulse to go into a bookstore. When you walk into the bookstore you may find that you are drawn to a certain table of books. You pick up one of the books, open it randomly and read a paragraph. Suddenly you realize that you are reading exactly what you need to hear at this moment in your life. In fact, this is the answer to the question you had asked that morning (although very often in these situations we forget that we had asked for exactly this piece of information).

Here's another example of how this can happen. You have a sudden impulse to call a friend you haven't heard from in a long time. In the course of the conversation your friend says something that has an impact, and helps you see a step that you need to take in your life. At some point you realize that you've been asking your inner guidance for clarity of direction and you've just received it.

Of course in these examples, it looks like the wisdom came from outside of you. But where did the impulse come from to walk into that bookstore and pick up that book? What made you call that friend? Something from within you prompted you to take those actions. Intuition is always trying to lead us in the direction we need to go, and it will use any method it can to help us.

Handling Special Problems

If you work with this meditation a while and don't feel that you are getting any stronger sense of connection with your intuition, here are some further suggestions that may help you.

You may be trying too hard to *make* something happen instead of simply *allowing* it to happen. You may be making the process into a bigger deal than it really is. Relax and let go. Stop trying to make anything amazing happen. Just listen a little more deeply than usual for your own sense of truth.

Try not to get caught up in needing to have an immediate answer. Life is an ongoing, unfolding process, and you may not be ready yet for a decision or a definite direction. You may be "in process." Inner guidance seldom gives us long-term information; it usually just lets us know what we need in the moment. Sometimes, inner guidance may be saying, "Just wait, don't do anything, allow yourself to be in confusion." When clarity is meant to come, it will.

If you feel really blocked for a long period of time, you probably need to do some emotional healing work. When we are holding our emotions inside us, it can be difficult or even impossible to contact our intuitive feelings. If you feel you may be having difficulties of this kind, find a good therapist or support group and begin the process of learning to experience and express your emotions. Once you've done a certain amount of deep emotional healing, you will automatically be more in touch with your intuition. (See chapter 9 for more information on this topic.)

Checking In on a Regular Basis

Once you have a little practice in relaxing, going inside, asking for an intuitive message, and paying attention to what comes to you either then or later, you can begin to integrate the process more naturally into your daily life.

In the middle of a busy day you may not have time to sit down and do a deep meditation. However you can learn to "check in" with your intuition on a regular basis throughout the day.

In order to do this, you need to develop the habit of pausing every now and then and taking a moment to notice what is going on inside of you.

Here is a quick, simple exercise that can help you touch in to your intuition even in the midst of a lot of activity. You can do this at your desk, or in a parked car briefly before or after you drive somewhere.

One excellent way to ensure a moment of quiet and privacy is to go into the bathroom to do this exercise. Of course, it's even better if you can take a minute to walk or sit outdoors; however, don't wait for that time if it is not going to happen easily. Just do it whenever and wherever you can.

QUICK INTUITIVE CHECK IN MEDITATION

Close your eyes and take a deep breath, exhaling slowly. Notice what's on your mind, what you've been thinking about. Notice how your body is feeling right now. How are you feeling emotionally? Do you feel like you are more or less "in the flow," following your own energy, or do you feel stressed, conflicted, out of sorts?

Take another deep breath, exhale slowly and let your awareness move into a deep place inside. Is there anything you need to pay attention to that would help you feel more connected to yourself? Any gut feeling you need to be aware of? Whether or not you get any specific information or awareness, enjoy a moment of rest before you carry on.

It doesn't matter too much what happens for you when you do this exercise. Just the fact that you are taking a moment to be with yourself and tune in on a deeper level will be very healing, and chances are that it will help you get more into the present moment. The more

66

present and connected with ourselves we are, the more likely we are to notice and follow our intuitive feelings, and the more effective we are likely to be in whatever we do.

To assist you in remembering to do this exercise, you can put little reminders where you are likely to see them around your work area and your home. A reminder can take the form of a little note to yourself, a poem, a picture, or an object that symbolizes or conveys to you a feeling of connecting to your intuition. You may want to put your reminders in different places every now and then, so that the reminders remain fresh and new and don't get overlooked and begin to blend into their surroundings.

Remember that our intuitive wisdom is always there inside of us and available. We may not always be able to access it, usually because we are too caught up in our activities, our minds, or our emotions. That's okay; it's just part of the cycles that we go through.

If you do this exercise or anything similar to it often, you will begin to build a relationship with your intuitive self and it will come through to you more and more frequently and clearly.

If we can develop the habit of checking our intuitive messages at least as often as most of us check our telephone messages, we'll be in great shape!

APPLYING THE INTUITIVE CHECK IN

You can apply the intuitive check in to many situations. Here's an example.

A few days ago one of my clients was driving to work and she got a flat tire. Her first impulse was to call her husband to come rescue her, but something inside her said, "Pause a moment, help is right there." She listened to this feeling, paused for a moment, observed her surroundings and within minutes was approached by a young couple willing and able to help her. Within twenty minutes she was on her way again.

If we can get into the habit of pausing, checking in with our inner guidance, we will often find answers to many of our questions, throughout the day.

CHAPTER SIX

Acting on Intuition

So far we've talked primarily about listening to intuition — learning how to access it and making a practice of paying attention to it as often as possible in our daily lives.

It's one thing to hear or sense our intuition, however, and another thing entirely to risk acting on what it tells us. This is where it can get quite challenging. We may wonder if we can really trust this gut feeling we're having enough to actually take action in practical, substantial ways. We fear that we might make a dreadful mistake. We may have other, conflicting voices and feelings going on inside.

One thing that can make it difficult to trust

and act on our intuitive feelings is that we usually only receive the piece of information we need right at the moment. It would be much easier if a wise person would come to us and explain exactly what we're supposed to do, and what results that action will have, and what to do after that. Or perhaps a scroll would roll down from heaven outlining our entire life plan and giving us long-term instructions. This would certainly make it easier for the part of us that wants to keep things carefully under control and know exactly what we're doing. Unfortunately, intuition rarely operates that way. It is true that we may occasionally get an intuitive glimpse of the future or of the big picture of our lives. This is more likely to happen as we become more intuitively developed. When it does happen, it can be extremely helpful and reassuring.

Most of the time, however, our intuitive sense operates moment by moment, giving us only the piece of information or the energetic nudge we need to take the appropriate action right now. If we keep following the energy, the next impulse will come to show us the next step. As we keep following our inner guidance, a path unfolds that takes us in the exact direction we need to go.

We can usually see this process much better in retrospect than we can at the time it's happening. At that time it feels like we are moving into the unknown, without knowing exactly what we're doing or why. We may feel uncertain and a bit afraid, yet excited and alive. It takes courage to keep taking those steps without knowing exactly where they will lead.

In learning to act on your intuition, it's very important to start practicing by taking small steps until you build trust and skill. It may be best not to make any major life decisions while you are in the initial learning stage! Don't quit your job suddenly because you think your intuition is telling you to. That message could be coming from another part of you. If you are just learning about following your intuition, try to postpone major decisions for a while until you've had more practice. If you have a major decision you must make, mull it over carefully, taking into account whatever intuitive feelings you may be having as well as all other factors.

Meanwhile, practice with small things, which incidentally are often more important and significant than we initially think. When you are faced with a simple choice or decision as you go through your day, such as what to wear, what route to drive, where to eat lunch, whether or not to call a friend, or which movie to see, briefly quiet your mind and go inside. Instead of making your choice on the basis of logical reasoning, what you think is "correct," or what others might feel, try to go by what your intuitive feeling tells you. Get in the habit of checking with your intuition and developing trust in yourself.

Make a practice, too, of noticing how you *feel* when you follow your intuition successfully and things are working out well. This will give you an internal reference point that can help you "click in" to your intuitive channel in the future. Soon you will become familiar with the feeling of your intuition.

If you get what seems like an intuitive feeling to take a certain action or move in a certain direction, and it's fairly easy and nondisruptive to do it, then give it a try. Do this in the spirit of adventure in order to better develop your intuitive ability.

For example, you hear about a speaker who's giving a lecture on a topic you know nothing

72

about, but you feel a little tingle of interest, so you go check it out. You may find that the topic is interesting and relevant to your life. Or you may hate the speaker and the topic, but run into an old friend that you're delighted to see. Or on your way to the lecture you may walk past a beautiful garden and get inspired to create a garden of your own. When following intuition you are never sure what the reward will be; it's often quite different than what you expect.

Another possibility with this example is that you may find no value in the experience at all, and wonder why you had the feeling to go. In learning to act on intuition, it's important to keep taking the feedback you get from the way things unfold. When we're truly following our intuition, things often have a way of working out smoothly or easily. Doors seem to open. The experience of going with your intuition is certainly not always smooth like this (and we will discuss this a little later), but it often is.

If you think you are following your intuition and yet things don't work out well, or you don't find much value in the experience you have, there are a number of possibilities. You may be misinterpreting or misunderstanding your inner guidance. You may be following a different feeling or voice that is actually not your intu-ition. Or, you may be following your intuition just fine, but it may be a more complex process than you expected, and perhaps you are not yet realizing the value of what's happening or where it will ultimately lead you.

Many years ago I fell in love with the Hawaiian island of Kauai. I rented a large house to lead a workshop there one summer, and then decided to buy a home there where I could live part time and hold retreats. I soon found a suit-able property for sale. The house was a bit odd in some ways, but I convinced myself that it would be okay. It had been on the market for a while and I made a good offer on it, so I felt confident that the sale would go through. I began to think of the house as mine, and I felt very happy and excited about it.

A few days later I learned that someone else had made a cash offer and bought the house right out from under me. I was totally shocked and dismayed. "My" house had been sold to another! I was very upset and felt that my intu-ition had misled me.

A short time later I found that the house I

was renting, although not officially on the market, was available at a very reasonable price. A contractor friend of mine showed me how it could be remodeled to perfectly suit my purposes. At that point I realized that the problems with the first house would have been much more serious than I had originally thought. In my eagerness to buy it, I had ignored my intuitive misgivings. So the "big disaster" actually saved me from a huge mistake, and my intuition then guided me to the right place. I bought the property and it became my beloved home for many years.

75

In the next few chapters we will discuss how you can fine-tune your ability to recognize, interpret, and act on your intuitive inner guidance. Meanwhile, don't take it too seriously and have some fun practicing with it.

CLEARING EXERCISE

Most of us have fears about what might happen if we act on our intuition. Take your notebook or a piece of paper and write down every reason you can think of why you are afraid or doubtful about acting on your intuitive feelings. Add to the list anytime you get in touch with another fear.

Writing down our fears helps us to clear them so that we can move forward.

TRUSTING YOURSELF EXERCISE

Here is an exercise that I would like to give you just for fun.

For one day, or for one week, or for some specific period of time that you choose, allow yourself to pretend or imagine that you are 100 percent right in whatever you intuitively feel. And for that period of time, act that way.

This is something I tried myself and it was wonderful. For just a period of time, I let go of my doubts and just assumed that whatever my intuition was telling me or whatever I thought my intuition was telling me was 100 percent right, and I acted upon it. I found that once I did that I wasn't really willing to go back to my old way of living ever again.

~ CHAPTER SEVEN ~

Interpreting Intuitive Messages

*I*t's not always easy to understand exactly what your intuition is saying or in what direction it is trying to move you. Your true intuition is always correct, but you may not always know how to interpret it correctly. The only way to develop that ability is to practice, and learn from everything that happens. You have to be willing to make some "mistakes," possibly to try something and "fail," perhaps even to feel foolish.

Keep in mind that although we often refer to our intuition as our "inner voice," it doesn't necessarily come to us as a voice speaking to us in words. We are more likely to experience it as a feeling —

perhaps a deep gut feeling, or a feeling of rightness or wrongness about something we are contemplating. Sometimes it may come as a kind of inner knowing about a particular topic or about our course of action. Often, our intuition may come to us in the form of energy, where we sense that our life energy is trying to move us in a certain direction, or is blocking us from moving in a certain way.

Intuition is seldom dramatic, grandiose, or particularly mystical. It's generally a very natural and normal feeling. It may be as simple as feeling, "I *want* to do this" or "I *don't want* to do that."

One of the most challenging aspects of developing your intuitive guidance is learning to distinguish your intuition from the other voices and energies within you. We'll explore that further in the next chapter.

No matter how long you have practiced following your intuition, there is almost always a feeling of uncertainty and risk involved. It rarely feels like a "sure thing." That is one reason that I advise beginning with small steps until you build enough confidence to deal with trusting your intuition in the larger issues of your life. On whatever level is appropriate for you, if you are willing to risk acting on what you sense is true for you, and risk making mistakes, you will learn very fast by paying attention to what works and what doesn't. If you hold back too much out of fear of being wrong, learning to trust your intuition could take a lifetime or longer!

To learn how to follow your intuition accurately, you have to try acting on what you believe is your intuition, and then see what the results are. Take in the feedback that life gives you, and learn from it.

Most often, when you are following your intuitive energy, you feel like you are "in the flow" of life. Things unfold smoothly and easily, opportunities open up, and you feel like you're in the right place at the right time doing the right thing. You may experience a sense of synchronicity with other people and events. Quite frequently things happen almost miraculously. You may even experience a profound sense of a higher power at work in the situation; it seems apparent that no individual human could have orchestrated things so perfectly.

A few years ago I was looking for someone

79

to work in my office. One evening I was leading a workshop near my home and I had an intuitive feeling that I should mention my need for an assistant, sensing that there might be someone in the group who would be suitable. I forgot to make the announcement, however, and only remembered it after the workshop was over and I was leaving. I felt annoyed with myself for forgetting, since I had had such a strong feeling that I would find the right person that evening.

As I walked outside, a woman who had been in the workshop approached me and asked if I by chance needed anyone to work for me! She had an intuitive feeling that she was meant to work with me. As it turned out, she had the right qualifications for the position. She later became my business manager, and we still work together today!

When things are unfolding smoothly and harmoniously like this, life is giving us great feedback that we are interpreting our intuition correctly and following it accurately.

Of course, it's not always this obvious and easy. Sometimes we find ourselves on a much bumpier road, where it can be confusing and difficult to tell whether we are truly following our inner guidance or not.

For one thing, our intuition often leads us down a very different path than we expected. It can be easy to assume that we are making a mistake because things don't go the way we planned or the way we think they ought to.

Our rational minds may think that we should proceed in a certain logical way from point A to point B to point C, whereas our intuition may guide us to skip point B altogether and arrive at point C through the back door! Or, even more disconcerting, we may never arrive at point C at all, but at point Z, which we never consciously knew existed as an option. Remember that through our intuition we have access to much more information than we have through our rational faculty.

Also, most of us hope that our path in life will be easy and we try to avoid difficulties and challenges. Because our inner guidance is always trying to take us in the direction of our greatest growth and development, it will sometimes lead us right into the challenge that we were hoping to avoid!

Suppose, for example, you are feeling unsatisfied in your job. You ask your intuition to

81

guide you in improving your work situation. You feel prompted to suggest some changes that could be made in your work place. Things seem to be improving. Suddenly, your boss announces that your department is downsizing and you are out of a job! You don't know where to look for another, or where money is going to come from. You are shocked and frightened, and wonder if the suggestions you made are the real reason you've been let go. Perhaps you made a terrible mistake in speaking up and trying to improve your situation!

After a couple of weeks of feeling paralyzed, you pull it together and start applying and interviewing for another job. However, nothing is inspiring you. One day your cousin calls to say he's coming into town with a friend and invites you to have lunch with them. His friend is opening a branch of his business in your city, you hit it off, and soon you have a new job that you love.

In many years of teaching people to follow their intuition I've heard countless stories like this, where something difficult or even seemingly disastrous happens that ultimately brings a wonderful result in a totally unexpected way.

Our intuition is always trying to get us where we need to go in the best possible way. Sometimes this involves letting go of things that we are very attached to, and it may feel as if our life is falling apart. If we are pushed to let go of something, it may be because we no longer need it, or it's time for it to change form.

When we look back on our lives, we can often see in retrospect why we had to go through certain difficulties, and how they ultimately led to our higher good. It's difficult to recognize this in the moment that something traumatic is happening, however. This is where the trust comes in. The more practice we have in following our intuition and seeing how things work out in the long run, the more trust in the process we develop.

If you feel uncertain about whether your intuition is guiding you to take a certain step or not, you can ask for greater clarity. You can say to your inner guidance, "Okay, I think this is what you want me to do, so I'm going to go ahead with this. If this is not right, please block it in some way. Give me a clear sign that this is not what I'm supposed to do."

Or you can do this process in reverse. You can say, "I think that you want me not to go forward with this. If you want me to do it, push me. Give me a clear sign that you want me to do this." If you ask for clarity in this way, you will usually get some type of further sign from within or without, or you will feel the energy moving or not moving.

Allowing Your Life Force to Flow

The surest and most reliable way to know whether you are following your intuition is that whenever you do so, you feel more alive! When you are listening to your intuitive feelings and acting on them, you keep your channel open so the life force can keep flowing. You literally have more energy moving through you.

When you don't pay attention to your intuition, or go against it, you may find that you feel a certain heaviness, lack of energy, a kind of deadness. This is because the life force is trying to come through and move you in a certain way, and it is being blocked.

When we aren't following the flow of our energy, life becomes a struggle. It's as if we are trying to swim upriver all the time. This is quite stressful and eventually takes a toll on our minds, emotions, and bodies. It also keeps us out of connection with our spiritual source.

On the other hand, the more we are able to move with the life force through following our inner guidance, the healthier and more vital our bodies become, the clearer and more relaxed our minds can be, and the more emotionally and spiritually fulfilled we feel.

A great way to practice developing your intuition is to notice whether following a certain inner prompting brings you a feeling of greater aliveness. Also notice whether there are times when you don't act on an intuitive feeling and you are left with a feeling of depression, numbness, loss of energy or power.

Suppose, for example, you are the kind of person who has a hard time expressing your opinions or feelings. You are in a conversation with someone and there is something you want to say, but you stop yourself out of fear and self-doubt. Afterward you notice that you are feeling depressed. Try not to criticize yourself for not speaking up. Just notice the lack of aliveness that you feel. Eventually it won't be worth it to you to feel that way, and you'll take the risk to speak your truth. Regardless of how the other person responds, and whatever emotions you may experience in the process, very likely you will feel enlivened and empowered by the experience.

On the other hand, if you are the type of person who always speaks your mind and expresses your thoughts and feelings, you may find yourself in a situation where your intuition tells you not to say anything. If you go ahead and follow your usual pattern of talking, you may experience a loss of energy. If you heed your intuition and keep quiet, you may find that you are left with a peaceful yet enlivened sense of self-containment.

Our inner guidance is always trying to lead us in the direction of greater self-development so it will sometimes prompt us to do the opposite of what we normally do. If we pay attention to what enlivens us, we often find that it comes from expressing different aspects of ourselves than we are accustomed to.

A student of mine, for example, was terrified of public speaking. His intuition prompted him to join Toastmasters. Once he got through his initial fear, he loved it!

The more you practice following your intuition the stronger it seems to get. As you pay attention to it more consistently it can come through to you louder and clearer.

Doing and Being

I have found that one of the most difficult challenges for most of us is when our intuition is telling us *not* to do something. We may have an idea about something we think we should be doing, and we find that there's simply no energy in it. We try to make ourselves do it, but it just doesn't work. In this situation we often think there is something wrong with us, and it may take a while to recognize that life is trying to give us the message that this is not the right course of action at the moment.

It can be even more disconcerting when we find that the energy doesn't seem to be moving in any direction at all. Nothing we try to do seems to work, or everything seems to require an enormous effort.

Our culture conditions us to believe that we must always be *doing* something outwardly productive. Many of us are extremely driven and feel that we must be accomplishing something at every moment. We have lost the value of being — taking time to rest, relax, contemplate, explore the inner realm, and generally replenish ourselves. We are terribly out of balance in this respect. I believe this is one reason why so many

87

people develop chronic fatigue syndrome and other related illnesses. Sometimes our bodies have to force us to stop driving ourselves.

Our intuition may be trying to show us how to develop the ability to relax and be present in the moment. Quite often, when people begin to pay attention to their inner guidance they go through a period of time where they don't feel like doing much for a while. This can be quite scary if they don't understand why it's happening. Many students and clients of mine have chosen to take a month, a few months, or even a year off work to give themselves space to rest and explore new possibilities. Obviously most people can't afford this, yet it always amazes me that when this is the right course of action for someone, it somehow works out financially. Once we surrender into a time of being — even if only for a few hours — and are replenished, our energy will again begin to move us into action, often in a new creative direction.

As we learn to listen to our intuitive feelings and act on them, we are truly learning to follow our own energy as it moves and rests. When we are receptive and responsive to this flow, it feels like the life force is moving us in an exquisite dance.

Energy Awareness Exercise

Make a practice of noticing how you feel and what happens to your energy when you follow your intuitive guidance and when you don't. Many people notice that their energy feels blocked or deadened when they don't act on their intuition, and more alive and flowing when they do. Is this true for you?

CHAPTER EIGHT

Distinguishing Intuition from Other Voices

Whenever I teach a group of people about developing intuition, invariably the question is asked, "How do I distinguish my intuition from all the other thoughts and feelings going on inside me?" This is a very important question to address.

Years ago, I used to refer to intuition as our "inner voice," until I began to realize that we actually have *many* voices inside of us. These voices are often in conflict with one another, and at times it can be quite confusing to sort out what is our intuition and what isn't. With practice, however, we can learn to distinguish the feeling or energy of our intuitive inner guidance from the other parts of us.

At about the time that I was trying to sort this all out, I was introduced to the work of Drs. Hal and Sidra Stone, creators of the Psychology of Selves and the powerful Voice Dialogue process. Their work was extremely helpful to me personally, and I have integrated it into my own teaching. The Stones have become important teachers and mentors of mine.

From Hal and Sidra I learned that we each have within our personality structure many different subpersonalities or "selves," and each one has its own distinct energy and voice.

Through the Voice Dialogue process we can learn to dialogue with these inner selves and discover why they are there, how they feel, and what they have to offer us. This can bring us a great deal of awareness about what is really going on inside of us, and can help us live much more consciously.

Our intuitive voice is one of these inner selves, and we are in the process of learning how to access that voice on a regular basis. It's not necessary to use Voice Dialogue in order to learn to distinguish your intuition from the other inner voices, but it can be helpful to understand more about the different selves within you.

The material I am presenting in this chapter is drawn from the Stone's work. I also highly recommend their books and tapes, which are listed in the "Recommended Resources" section.

We are all born as microcosms of the universe with an infinite number of different archetypal qualities or energies within us. One of our most important tasks in life is to develop and express as many of these energies as possible so that we can be well-rounded and experience the full range of our potential. In a way it's as if there are many different characters living inside of us, each with its own task and purpose.

Each of us has developed certain of our inner selves very highly. These are the ones that we are very identified with, and the ones that we present to the world. These are our *primary selves*. There are certain other selves that we are afraid of, ashamed of, or in some way uncomfortable about, and we try to keep them hidden. These are called *disowned selves*, and they make up what Carl Jung called the "shadow side" of our personality.

If you are identified with being strong, self-sufficient, and hardworking, for example, then some of your primary selves would probably be the voice of power, the independent self, and the pusher (the one who drives us to accomplish our goals and achieve success). Your disowned selves are probably the opposites of these energies — the vulnerable child, for example, and perhaps the "beach bum" or one who enjoys just relaxing and being.

Our primary selves are generally making most of our decisions and running our lives. Their purpose is to try to keep us safe and make us acceptable to others and as successful as possible. They are usually trying pretty hard to keep our disowned selves hidden and under control, since they fear that the disowned energies will be harmful to us or disrupt our lives. Most of us have very little awareness of all of this; it's going on inside us fairly unconsciously.

94

The truth is that all of our energies — primary and disowned — are essential parts of us. We need them all in order to experience wholeness and fulfillment.

If you are overly identified with action and achievement, for example, you need to develop the opposite polarity — relaxation and play — in order to create balance. If you are a very giving person, you probably need to learn to receive.

How do we become conscious of the many selves within and bring them into balance in our lives?

The first and most important step is to begin to recognize and become aware of our primary selves. What qualities and energies are you most identified with? Can you begin to notice the selves within you that automatically make most of your decisions and run your life?

For example, if you are the kind of person who is very sensitive to other people's needs and feelings, and often find yourself giving to others, your "caretaker" is probably one of your primary selves. If so, you may often find yourself auto-matically taking care of someone without really making a conscious decision to do so. Your care-taker self just jumps in and does its thing without much awareness on your part. Once you become conscious of this process, you can have more choice in the matter.

We want to honor and appreciate our pri-mary selves for how much they've done for us, and yet separate a bit from being totally identi-fied with them. As soon as we become conscious of them as *energies within us* rather than *who we are*, we are beginning to develop what is called *aware ego.* Aware ego is the ability to recognize and hold all the different selves within us, so that we can have conscious choice about which ones we bring through at any given moment.

Once we have some awareness in relation to our primary selves, the disowned selves start to come forth. The primary selves usually remain our strongest qualities, but we begin to feel more balanced and our lives start to work better as we begin to integrate the energy from previously disowned selves. The disidentification with the primary selves, the development of aware ego, and the acknowledging of the disowned selves is a gradual process that happens over a lifetime. Every step we take in this process, however, can make a big difference in our lives.

Our intuitive wisdom is one of the energies or selves within us. If you were encouraged to trust your intuition at an early age, or had an intuitive parent figure as an early role model, or for whatever reason are simply a more "right-brained" type of person, your intuition may be a primary self. Since our culture tends to deny or devalue the intuitive function, however, for a majority of people it is a disowned or relatively

96

underdeveloped self, while rationality is often one of the primary selves.

If rationality is a primary self, and intuition is disowned, we may need to separate from over-identification with our rational side in order to get in touch with our inner guidance. We do this by recognizing our rational side as one aspect of who we are, and beginning to notice how it operates in our lives. Once we become more aware of it in this way, we are no longer so identified with it and we can begin to have more conscious choice about how and when we use it. This creates space to explore our intuitive side as well.

If intuition is a primary self, we may have difficulty thinking logically or dealing with practical matters in a grounded way. In this case, we may need to develop our rational, practical side in order to ground our intuition in the physical world.

As we are learning to distinguish our intuition from other energies, it can be helpful to know some of the other selves. Here are some of the most common ones. Some of them may be primary selves for you, and some of them may be disowned selves.

97

The Rational Mind	Intuition
The Responsible Self	The Free Spirit
The Caretaker	The Perfectionist
The Vulnerable Child	The Playful Child
The Doer or Pusher	Being
The Rule Maker	The Rebel
Self-Acceptance	The Critic
The Straight Talker	The Pleaser

As you begin to recognize some of these energies inside of you, you can learn to distinguish them from your intuition. For example, if there's a part of you feeling that you *should* take a particular action, that is probably your inner rule maker or perfectionist, not your intuition. If you are feeling self-critical or judgmental of others, that is your inner critic or judge, definitely not your intuitive voice. Intuition never guides us with an authoritarian or critical edge. It doesn't impose rules, it never feels heavy handed or burdensome, it doesn't push us to anything that we're really not ready to do, and it never makes us feel guilty about anything. It's also not self-indulgent or rebellious, and never leads us to do something that isn't good for us physically or emotionally. These feelings come from other parts of ourselves. Our intuitive guidance brings a feeling of enlivenment, openness, even sometimes relief and release. It feels good in our heart and soul. It feels like exactly the right step to take in the moment.

False Cravings and Addictions

It's very important to distinguish between our false cravings or addictions and our true intuitive impulses. One takes us down a familiar road that we know is ultimately futile and painful. The other leads us in a new direction that is satisfying and enlivening.

A false craving is something we think we want, but when we get it, it doesn't really satisfy us or enhance our lives. We are lured by false cravings when we are not conscious of our true needs and desires, or when we don't know how to fulfill them.

When we pursue a false craving to the point where we become obsessive and out of control, it becomes an addiction. An addiction appears to satisfy some of our needs momentarily, but not for long, because it does not address our real needs. In fact, an addiction causes an increasing

99

amount of damage and destruction to our lives and the lives of those around us.

One of the most damaging things about addiction is that it very effectively keeps us from getting in touch with and learning to satisfy our true needs and desires. For that reason, and many others, if we hope to create anything in our lives, we must first acknowledge and begin to heal any addictive patterns we may have. And most of us do have them, to one degree or another.

In this day and age, most of us are aware of a virtual epidemic of drug and alcohol addiction in our society. Also, we are becoming aware of how many of us suffer from serious eating disorders such as anorexia and bulimia. Other forms of common addictive behavior include sexual addiction, various forms of obsession about relationships, workaholism, compulsive shopping, and gambling.

Some of these are more subtle than others, and some, like work addiction, are so supported by society they may be difficult to recognize as addictive behavior. Even meditation can become an addiction for some. Anything we do habitually to avoid the pain of not having our real needs met can be an addiction.

100

Our addictions are ways we unconsciously try to fill the emptiness we feel inside. This emptiness can only be filled by the things we truly need, such as a deep connection to our spiritual source, a close relationship with nature, loving contact with other humans, satisfying work, and a sense of making a contribution. In order to fill those needs, we must allow ourselves to feel them.

An addiction is not something to be ashamed of, although most of us are. We all have them in one form or another. The great thing is that when our addictive behavior becomes painful and self-defeating enough, it forces us to begin or deepen our healing process.

We are fortunate enough to live in a time when many resources exist to help and support us in this process. The twelve-step programs such as Alcoholics Anonymous, Al-Anon, Overeaters Anonymous, Gamblers Anonymous, Debtors Anonymous, and so forth are a very effective way for many people to deal with an addictive process. There are also many therapists and support groups that specialize in these issues. If you think you might have an addiction problem, I urge you to reach out for the appropriate help. It could be the most important step toward health and happiness you ever take!

(It's good to note, as a dear friend of mine who is a recovering alcoholic likes to say, if you think you might have an addiction, you probably do — if you didn't, you'd never think about it, would you?)

Our intuitive self has a unique energy or feeling, and we can learn to recognize and distinguish it from all the other voices inside us. Many of our other voices seem to be located primarily in our head, whereas our intuitive feelings usually seem to come through a deeper place in our bodies. The following exercises may help you distinguish your intuitive energy from some of the others.

BECOMING AWARE OF YOUR SELVES EXERCISE

Sit in a comfortable position and close your eyes. See if you can become aware of any "selves" that are with you right now, or any voices that are going on in your head. Do you have any sense of who they are? What are they feeling or saying to you? Take a few minutes to be with them and listen to them. See if you can identify any of them from the list I gave you earlier.

Now take several long, slow deep breaths, and imagine moving your attention out of your head and dropping it slowly down to a deeper place in your body — your heart, your solar plexus, or your belly. Imagine that your wise, intuitive self lives in there. Ask if it has any message for you — a feeling, a thought, or an image. Be receptive to whatever comes to you.

Sit with it for a few minutes. When you feel complete, get up and go about your life.

EXPRESSING DIFFERENT VOICES EXERCISE

If you are feeling a lot of inner conflict about an issue or a decision you need to make, try this exercise:

Get several pens with different colors of ink, and a pad of paper or your journal. Sit in a comfortable position and close your eyes. Get in touch with some of the different voices that are going on inside you. Choose one of the voices to express, and pick up a pen to represent that voice. Let it write anything it wants to say.

Then choose another voice, and a different colored pen. Write anything that voice wants to say.

For example, if you are trying to decide whether to make a particular change in your life, you might use a black pen to express the conservative voice in you that thinks it's unwise to make this change, a red pen to express the risk-taking voice that wants to do something new and different, a blue pen to express the vulnerable child in you who is afraid of the change (or who may want the change), a green pen to express your creative voice, and so on.

Continue this until the major voices have gotten a chance to express themselves. You may find that some of them are directly in opposition to others. Don't try to find a resolution right now. Just be aware of all the different feelings and points of view inside of you.

Then take a few slow deep breaths and let your attention move down into a deep place inside. Ask your intuition if there's anything you need to be aware of right now. Be receptive to whatever comes to you. If nothing comes right now, that's okay too.

When you feel complete for now, get up and go about your life.

Don't try to resolve anything or make a decision right away. Chances are that some clarity about this issue or this decision will begin to come to you within a few days or a week or two.

105

CHAPTER NINE

Intuition and Emotions

What is the relationship between our intuition and our emotions? We use the word "feeling" to describe both our intuitive promptings and our emotions. It can be easy to confuse the two. Our intuitive feelings and our emotional feelings are different, yet they are closely related.

As we discussed in the last chapter, we have many different "selves" within us. One of those is our intuitive self. Certain other selves carry our emotional feelings. For example, we all have within us a vulnerable, sensitive child who carries our emotional needs. That part of us can easily feel hurt, sad, or scared. It is also capable of giving and receiving deep love and affection, and creating real intimacy in our relationships. We have a playful child within us as well, one who knows how to have fun and enjoy life. We also have a self that gets angry and tries to defend us when we feel hurt or afraid. So there are really a number of parts of us that carry various emotions.

Any of these parts may be a primary self or a disowned self. If it's a primary self, it is one we identify with and show to the world. If it is a disowned self we usually bury it or hide it. We may not even know that we have it, or if we do we may feel ashamed and embarrassed about it.

108

Many people have disowned almost all of their emotions. They pride themselves on being tough and strong, or they approach everything rationally. They may not feel many emotions and when they do, they hide them. They may have difficulty creating real connection and intimacy with others.

Some people have their emotional parts as primary selves. These people are extremely sensitive and highly emotional. They may have difficulty setting boundaries and creating stability in their lives. They often feel and express other people's emotions as well as their own. If they don't take care of themselves they can become victims.

Most of us feel comfortable with some of our emotions but not others. Certain emotional selves are primary, while others are disowned. For example, some people — especially many men — feel okay about showing their anger, but are extremely uncomfortable showing any vulnerable feelings. Other people — especially many women — can express their fear or sadness, but are afraid to show any anger. Many people are in touch with the playful child within them, but disown the more vulnerable child.

109

The healthiest and most balanced way to live is to be in touch with all our emotions, and know how and when to express them appropriately. To live life fully, we need to allow ourselves to feel deeply and passionately, yet not be constantly overwhelmed by our emotions. For most of us, this takes some work and healing on the psychological level.*

Any emotions that we deny and disown tend to remain inside us as blocked energy.

*For more understanding of the emotional healing process, I suggest reading my book *The Four Levels of Healing* (or listening to the tape).

These energies can build up over years and eventually cause emotional and physical problems.

While our intuition is not the same as our emotions, it is very intimately connected with them. In a sense, intuition lies underneath our emotions. When we shut down our emotions, it's much more difficult to connect with our intuition. The more we allow ourselves to be in touch with our emotional feelings and express them appropriately, the easier it is to be in touch with our intuitive feelings. When we are "in the flow" emotionally, our intuition comes through more easily.

110

One reason that women are often considered to be more intuitive than men is that women have been more culturally supported to be in touch with their emotions. Since they are generally more comfortable in the inner realm of feelings, it is easier for many women to stay in touch with their intuition. (Interestingly enough, however, it is often difficult for women to trust themselves enough to *act* on their intuitive feelings.)

Men, on the other hand, have traditionally been conditioned to disconnect from their feelings in order to deal with the challenges of the external world. Since men have not been allowed to feel very much, it can be more difficult for some men to access their intuition. Fortunately these stereotypes are rapidly dissolving. In my own experience, with a little practice and encouragement most men can develop their intuition just as easily as most women.

Once we are aware of our emotional feelings, it is not too difficult to distinguish them from our intuitive feelings. Each emotion has its own particular energy, and our intuition has a unique energetic vibration. We may feel our emotions and our intuition differently in our bodies (see the next chapter on "Intuition and the Body").

The more emotional healing we've done and the clearer we are with our emotions, the more likely it is that our emotions and our intuitive feelings will go hand in hand. We will feel a yearning to go in a certain direction in life, and that will be coming from both the emotional and the intuitive level. Or we may feel emotionally and intuitively uncomfortable about something and realize that it's just not right for us.

If we have disowned our emotions, or in

some way are out of balance in our emotional lives, how do we do our emotional healing work?

In general, we need someone supportive that we can talk to honestly about our feelings. If we have friends or family that we can be truly authentic with, that may be enough. I have found, however, that most of us need some professional help from a counselor, psychotherapist, or support group, at least at some point in our lives.

112

Many of us feel ashamed at the thought of needing emotional support, because our culture so strongly emphasizes self-sufficiency. It is truly a mark of strength, however, to be willing to admit that we have things to learn.

If you sense that you have some blocked emotions that may be interfering with your ability to access your intuition, or with your ability to find fulfillment in life, I strongly recommend that you try working with a good therapist for a period of time.

There are many different kinds of therapists with a wide range of effectiveness. Don't be afraid to shop around. Try to find someone who really helps you get in touch with and express your feelings honestly and authentically. (One possibility is to find a Voice Dialogue facilitator in your area, which you can do by contacting Hal and Sidra Stone's office, listed in the "Recommended Resources" section.)

GETTING IN TOUCH WITH EMOTIONS EXERCISE

When you wake up in the morning, close your eyes and put your attention in the middle of your body — your heart, your solar plexus, and your abdomen. Ask yourself how you are feeling emotionally right now. Try to distinguish your feelings from the thoughts you are having in your head. Are you feeling peaceful, excited, anxious, sad, angry, joyful, frustrated, guilty, loving, lonely, fulfilled, serious, playful?

If there seems to be an anxious or upset feeling inside of you, go into that feeling and give it a voice. Ask it to talk to you and tell you what it's feeling. Make an effort to hear it and listen to its point of view. Be sympathetic, loving, and supportive toward your feelings. Ask what you can do to take care of yourself at this time.

Repeat this exercise before you go to sleep at night, and at any other time during the day that feels appropriate.

CHAPTER TEN

Intuition and the Body

One way to get in touch with your intuition is to get more in touch with your physical body. Your body is a tremendous helper in learning to follow your inner wisdom.

One of the ills of modern society is that we tend to be disconnected from our bodies. We spend a lot of time in our intellect, always thinking, trying to figure everything out, and ignoring the body's messages. The body is often trying in subtle or not so subtle ways to guide us toward getting our needs met.

I recently took a day off to relax and nurture myself at a beautiful hot springs resort near my home. I was lying in a lovely spot under a tree, resting and meditating. I soon became aware that I could hear people talking nearby. I tried to ignore it, since I really liked this spot and didn't know where else I could go that would be as restful. My mind told me that I could just ignore the bothersome noise. After a few minutes, however, my body felt tight and tense. I kept thinking about a trail I had seen. I followed what my body wanted to do — I got up and began to walk up the trail. In a short time I came to a beautiful meadow with no one around. I lay down, and this time was able to relax deeply. My intuition had come through my body to guide me to the perfect place to enjoy the silence I was craving.

The more you *feel* your body and *listen* to the signals that your body is giving you, the more it helps you get connected to your intuition. Meditation helps you do this, especially if you can drop your awareness from your head into your solar plexus area or your heart. Focusing on those parts of your body will help you get out of the intellect and into your intuitive self.

Intuition can be experienced in the body in many ways. Some people feel their intuition in their solar plexus — often referred to as a "gut feeling." Some people feel it through their heart or through their hands. Other people get goose bumps whenever something is said that rings true for them; some may feel like they are being physically pulled in a particular direction by a magnet.

I know a woman who goes through a check-list in her mind when she gets feelings of anxiety, and if the anxiety flares up in her body as she's going through her list, she knows what to put her attention on. Her list is something like this:

Work	Children	Husband
Exercise	House	Garden
Finances	Travel	Parents

She meditates for ten to fifteen seconds on each subject on her list and then moves on to the next subject. Should the anxiety level in her body increase on any of the subjects, she then knows she needs to pay attention to it. If her anxiety increases in her body on the word "work," for instance, she then creates another list that covers all the projects she's currently working on. And she eventually locates the project that is causing her the anxiety, and she gives it the attention that it needs. This system of identifying something has been very helpful in eliminating unnecessary feelings of inadequacy and confusion for her. She has come up with a great way to listen to her body and use the information she receives on a daily basis.

Listening to Your Body

The body is a very powerful messenger. When you get sick, for example, it is often because your intuition is trying to show you something or trying to reach you in some way. It is often telling you to slow down, to relax, to take better care of yourself, to listen to yourself, and to trust yourself more.

Often when I'm working on a project my intuition lets me know I'm going in the right direction when I feel excitement run through my body. Other times, I know I'm on the right track because I feel peaceful, content, and calm. These are just two examples of how my body communicates with me everyday. Once we are aware of these sensations, we can follow the intuitive impulses we receive through our bodies quite easily.

A friend of mine once told me that she started to notice her intuition working through her body about twenty years ago. She had been invited to go to a barbecue with a new male friend. (She had been divorced from her ex-husband for a couple of years and was beginning to date again.) She had been looking forward to this afternoon barbecue all week long, but the day of the event, she woke up with an uneasy feeling in her body. She didn't know what it was, she just felt something was wrong. She went to the barbecue, and for the most part had a good time, but the uneasy feeling never quite left her. As her new friend was driving her home she began to explain the feelings of anxiety that had been with her all day. They arrived home, put away the softball equipment they had taken to the barbecue, and then the doorbell rang. She opened the door and was handed a subpoena — her ex-husband had defaulted on an old credit card debt and *she* was being sued because she had been on the account, years earlier, and the bank was unable to find her ex-husband. As soon as she received the subpoena, the uneasy feeling was gone — she now knew what was "wrong." She had *felt it coming* all day.

She recognized, from that experience, that her body was "picking up something" — trying to tell her something. Since then, she has paid careful attention to the intuitive messages she gets through her body and has learned how to use the information in her daily life.

JOURNAL EXERCISE

Here is a journal exercise that may help you to be more aware of intuitive feelings in your body.

Over a period of at least a week, make a note in your journal every time you experience an intuitive impulse or hunch through your body. For example, you may feel unusual and unexplained excitement on your way to work, or you may have a strong feeling of concern that you are forgetting something as you leave the house. Keep a record of the feelings that come to you through your body, and also keep a record of the times when your intuitive feelings were validated. For example, getting to work and receiving a beautiful delivery of flowers for no particular reason or getting an unexpected raise would validate the unexplained excitement you experienced on your way to work.

The more you practice recognizing this type of experience through your body the easier it will become to recognize your intuition. Your ability to use your intuition on a daily basis will increase.

Intuition and Health

The body is a great messenger, although it's not always easy to interpret what your body is trying to tell you. Relaxing, releasing, and meditating can help you feel your inner guidance working through your body.

Often the body speaks amazingly clearly and metaphorically: a woman whose back aches because she's carrying too much responsibility, for example, or a man who has a heart attack because he's pushing so hard that he's ignoring the needs of his own heart.

Understanding what your body is trying to tell you may not always be easy. It requires time to cultivate your ability to listen, and it can be helped by quiet contemplation, journal writing, or therapy.*

*For further information on the subject of physical, emotional, mental, and spiritual health, read *The Four Levels of Healing*.

Don't worry if you don't understand with your mind what your body is trying to communicate right away. If you are open, you will eventually get the messages your body is trying to give you. Also, be careful not to accept anyone else's interpretation of what your body is trying to tell you unless it feels right to you!

It is important to recognize and become aware of the intuitive impulses we receive in our bodies, and to trust these impulses. If we are not aware, however, our bodies will find ways to get our attention. This often happens through "accidents" or illness.

Not long ago one of my business associates experienced her body getting her attention in a very dramatic way. She has always been a very busy person — able to accomplish enormous amounts of work in her typical twelve- to fourteen-hour day. She had a lot of energy, loved her work, and was very good at what she did. Many years of working at this fast-paced level, however, began to wear on her body, mind, and soul.

She kept getting intuitive messages that she needed to take some time off to rest and replenish her body. However, her inner "pusher" kept driving her to accomplish more. She began to get ill, nothing too serious, but it seemed that any cold that was going around would find its way to her. She never quite recovered from one cold or flu before she came down with another. Instead of listening to her body and resting, she worked more hours a day to make up for her slower pace due to the illnesses.

Eventually, her body became exhausted, her responses slowed. She was in an automobile accident and had a concussion. Again, she felt that if she worked more hours she could keep up with her work, and she attempted to do so. Of course, this didn't work either. Eventually, she was in another accident and this time she suffered slight brain damage. She *had* to stop. Her body was trying to tell her to slow down, that she needed a break, and she needed to rest. Eventually she took some time off work and got the rest she needed, and has learned how to create balance in her life.

This is an extreme example of the body sending messages that were being ignored. It's not necessary for any of us to experience such a drastic way for our bodies to communicate with us. The trick is to become aware and pay attention to your body and what it may be trying to say to you.

BODY TALK EXERCISE

To become aware of your body as an intuitive message sender or to improve on an
awareness you may already have developed,
here is a simple exercise you can do. This exercise can be repeated each day or each week if
you like.

Sit or lie down in a comfortable position.
Take a deep breath. Feel yourself sink into the
floor or chair. Take another deep breath and feel
the weight of your body connect with the
ground, and feel supported by the earth below
you. Gradually allow your mind to grow quiet.
Take another deep breath and let your body feel
like it is being held and protected, surrounded
by light and warmth.

Take another deep breath and ask your
body, "What would you like to tell me at this
time?" If you are troubled with a particular illness or with aches and pains, ask your body
specifically what the illness or aches are trying
to tell you. Be patient and breathe deeply.

As you inhale, allow your body to feel the
nurturing, healing properties of the oxygen
you take in, and when you exhale release any

discomfort or anxiety. As you do this, bring yourself into a deeper place within your body. Notice any feelings, sensations, and images you may receive as you do this exercise.

Now ask your body, "How can I help relieve these concerns?" Again, notice any feelings, sensations, and images.

Now, take a deep breath and thank your body for the information it has given you. When you feel comfortable and ready, open your eyes and make some notes in your journal about the information you received.

Be sure to make note of how your body communicated the information to you. Did you experience goose bumps, a sense of calm, anxiety, thoughts, or images? Did you get stomach cramps or feel like falling asleep? Noting how your body communicated to you will give you some valuable information. If you felt like falling asleep, your body may be trying to communicate that you need more rest, or you may need to do this exercise at a different time when you are more *able* to be with the exercise.

Only you will know what your body is communicating to you, depending on your particular situation.

CHAPTER ELEVEN

Intuition and Work

*I*ntuition can be a great aid in your work, as in every other area of your life. Using intuition can help you process information, make decisions, take better care of yourself, and interact with people more successfully. Bringing the tool of intuition into your work life can make your day more efficient, enjoyable, and even effortless at times.

On a deeper level, following your intuitive guidance supports your creative expression, helps you create work you love, and brings you satisfaction and success on all levels, financial and otherwise. I often read interviews, articles, and biographies of well-known people and I've found that most successful people have trusted and followed their intuition on a regular basis or at key moments in their lives.

For some people it can be especially difficult to pay attention to their intuitive feelings in the workplace because the atmosphere there may not feel supportive of that process. Traditionally most businesses and institutions have been run on a patriarchal model that left little room for the intuitive process. Fortunately, many businesses are beginning to recognize and support the value of intuition.

It can be challenging to maintain your integrity and stay true to yourself in a work environment, but it can have big rewards. Here is a rather dramatic story that illustrates this.

One of my close friends was hired a couple of years ago as the chief operating officer for a midsize corporation. Last year, during a top management meeting, the company decided to make some internal changes, and they felt that they should keep the information quiet and not tell the union. My friend intuitively knew that keeping this information from the union was the wrong strategy and he was adamant about being honest and open with the union. He felt strongly that keeping the information "secret" was inappropriate and would create feelings of mistrust.

He knew he was going out on a limb by being the only one in the management team to disagree with the secrecy; however, he felt strongly that honesty was best and would serve them all in the long run. He adamantly told the management team he would take full responsibility if something went wrong, and he was finally able to convince them to allow him to share their changes with the union. Initially there was chaos, as everyone's fears came out. Soon, however, the management team and the union started working together to create a vision for the company. The company's profits went from $3 million to $33 million in one year.

Intuition can be a fantastic guide to finding the right job at any stage along your journey. When following your intuition on a job search, things often happen in surprising and synergistic ways.

A few years ago, my business manager, Lora, was talking to a friend, Gina, who mentioned that she intuitively felt they would work together some day. They agreed that they both liked the idea but had no idea how that might happen, as they were in quite different fields at the time.

About a year ago we were in a staff meeting and one of our part-time employees gave notice that she was leaving and going on to other things. During that meeting, Gina just "happened" to call and leave a message for Lora mentioning that she was currently looking for work and asking for the phone number of a possible job contact. Lora mentioned the job at our office that had just become available, but Gina needed a full-time position. A week later, another part-time employee of ours decided to go back to school. Now we could offer Gina a full-time position; however she was overqualified for the job and the salary was lower than she needed. Still, she intuitively felt she wanted to take the job anyway. She proved to be a great asset to our company, and within six months she created a management position with a more appropriate salary.

When we talked about how remarkably everything had fallen into place, this question came up: "Was this following intuition, or was this synchronicity?" My feeling is that synchronicity happens as a result of following intuition.

Your intuition is a wonderful guide to help you discover and create work that you love and find fulfilling. Remember, though, that intuition can only guide you as fast as you are ready to go, and often there is much to learn along the way, so the process of finding your right livelihood may take time and go through many different stages. Since intuition guides us step-by-step, we have to be willing to take those steps without necessarily knowing where they are going!

A woman in my two-year program decided to quit her long-time job managing an automobile dealership. This was a very scary step for her, as she was used to the security of her position. She had an intuitive feeling that there was something else she wanted to do but had no idea what it was. She took a few months off to rest and contemplate. During her time off, she found that her most enjoyable time was spent playing with her two dogs. Since she lived on a large property, she got the idea to start a "doggie daycare" business, just for fun. Within a few months she had a highly successful business doing something she loves — playing with dogs. Now she is trying to decide whether to keep expanding the business, or keep it small and simple. As long as she keeps following her intuition, it's certain she will find what is best for her.

Intuition and Money

When we trust and follow our intuition, life tends to support us in that process in various ways, including financially. Money is fundamentally a symbol of energy, and it reflects how energy is moving in our lives. When we are following the flow of our energy and taking the steps that are right for us, money usually flows through our lives in an appropriate amount to take care of our responsibilities and do the things we need to do.

Everyone has different needs and destinies in relation to money. Some people lead relatively simple lives and only require a modest amount of money; others have more complex lives and require larger amounts of money. My feeling is that when we follow our intuition, we are provided with enough money to accomplish our life purposes.*

Here is a remarkable example of someone taking the risk to follow his intuitive feelings in the face of common sense, with high stakes involved:

*There is much to be said about the relationship of intuition and money, and I have written about it more extensively in my book *Creating True Prosperity*.

132

I know a man from New York City who married a woman in California just over a year ago. When they married they had decided that living together in California was their goal. The man just needed to finish up a few things in his current job and would then begin to look for work in California. He was in a field that easily allowed him to work on either coast.

He started pursuing positions in California, and not long into his search he was offered what appeared to be a fabulous partnership with a company just minutes from their new home. The company was very successful, and their offer was quite attractive.

Over the next four months, however, he kept putting off making the decision to join the company. His energy would drop every time he picked up the phone to talk with one of the partners. He couldn't quite put his finger on why he always seemed exhausted just thinking about working with them. After many long discussions with his wife, he still wasn't able to articulate why he kept putting off the decision to join the West Coast company, except that he had a "gut feeling" he needed to stay put for the time being. His wife was in touch with her intuitive feelings and understood how powerful a "gut feeling" can be, and accepted the delay in their being together in California. The man turned down the position and continued to work with the company he was with in New York.

As it turned out, the company in New York did a public offering just six months later and he, as an officer of the company, made millions of dollars. Though he and his wife had to put off living together for a little over a year, they are both grateful that they listened to his inner guidance and trusted enough that *not* doing something was the right thing to do.

Intuition and Your Higher Purpose

Almost everyone, at some point, questions what life is about and why they are here. As you develop your intuition you will begin to experience subtle changes in your life. These changes may lead you to examine your life with new eyes.

Every one of us comes into this life with lessons to learn and gifts to give. The more we learn and grow, the more we become capable of developing and sharing these natural gifts. As we develop our intuition, we find ourselves guided toward discovering and fulfilling our higher purpose in life. That higher purpose is, quite literally, the sharing of our gifts.

Most of us grew up believing that when we became adults, we had to decide what our career would be and then pursue an education or take other steps to achieve that career. That chosen career would then be what we did to earn a living for most, or all, of our life.

Today, many of us do a number of things that come together in fascinating combinations. As you practice following your intuition, it may lead you in many directions. You may express yourself in a variety of areas, all of which will begin to synthesize in some surprising, interesting, and very new, creative way. You'll be doing what you love, what you're good at, what comes easily to you and has an element of challenge and excitement to it. Whatever you do will feel satisfying and fulfilling to you. Everything you do becomes a contribution.

Your fantasies can tell you a great deal about yourself. Many times, I've found that people have a strong sense of what they would like to do, yet they take up a career that is very different from their desires. Sometimes they go for the opposite because they feel it is practical or will gain the approval of their parents or their peers. They figure it is impossible to do what they really want, so they might as well settle for something else that comes along. I encourage people to risk exploring the things that really turn them on. Here is an example:

A friend of mine worked in the medical insurance business. Although she made a good living, she felt unfulfilled and wanted to find her life's work. She was very successful with insurance; in fact, the owner of the company offered her a partnership because she had tripled his business in the short time she had worked with him. In considering the partnership offer, she began working with a personal counselor. Her counselor led her through some meditations and exercises to help her discover what she was truly passionate about. Eventually she turned down the partnership offer. She knew she could make a lot of money selling insurance, but that particular type of work did nothing to nourish her soul.

By working with her counselor, she discovered that she really wanted to work with troubled teens. She had struggled as a teenager herself and wanted to offer teens in her community a place to gather and discuss issues that concerned them — a place where they could learn the tools they needed to build their self-esteem. Although she didn't know how it was going to take place, she knew that working with teens was where she wanted and needed to be.

She continued to work in the insurance business to support herself, and began volunteer work with a nonprofit organization in her community called Students for Self-Esteem. The first year she was involved with the organization she was asked to join the executive committee, and the second year she was asked to be the executive director — a paying position. She was finally able to give up the insurance job and work full time for the nonprofit organization. She ran the program for several years before moving from the community to work with an even larger audience in the personal growth area of the publishing industry, where she has specialized in helping to produce a growing line of books for teenagers and young adults. She has felt blessed to work with the authors she has met over the years and takes a great deal of pride in helping bring their work to larger audiences.

This is just one story of many that people have shared with me. The woman in the story above wasn't willing to "settle" for a career that didn't bring her any personal fulfillment or joy, even though she could make a lot of money and feel financially secure. Not having the background to get into the field she desired to be in, she found a way to get involved through volunteer work. This approach enabled her to fulfill her passion to work with teens and eventually launched her into a career in publishing.

As you experiment and develop your intuitive skills, you will connect more deeply with your own soul and the energy of the universe. Your worldview may begin to change and these changes may lead you on your own unique path to discover your purpose in life.

138

EXERCISES FOR DISCOVERING YOUR PASSION

1. Follow any impulses you have in the direction of your true work/play/creative desires. Even if it seems totally unrealistic, follow the impulse anyway in the spirit of openness and adventure, and see what happens.

2. List any fantasies you've had around work, career, or creativity, and beside that list,

make another list of the action steps you plan to take to explore these fantasies.

3. Write an "ideal scene" — a description of your perfect job or career exactly as you would like it to be. Write it in the present tense, as if it were already true. Put in enough description and details to make it seem very real. Put it away somewhere, and look at it again in a few months or even a year or two. Unless your fantasy has changed completely in that time, chances are you will find you have made significant progress in the direction of your dream.

139

4. Cut out pictures you come across or articles that pertain to your desires and collect them in a large envelope to help you develop a clearer picture of what you would like to create for yourself. This can be fun to look at every month or so, to see if you can see anything emerging or a clue about what direction to take.

Alternatively, you can glue the pictures into a notebook, or onto a piece of poster board to create a collage to hang on your wall. Look at it often and let it inspire you.

CHAPTER TWELVE

The Art of Following Intuition

*L*istening to, trusting, and acting on your intuitive inner guidance is an art. Like any other art or discipline, it requires a certain commitment. It is an ongoing process in which we are always being challenged to move to a deeper level of self-trust.

For most of us, the practice of allowing our intuition to guide us is really a new way of life, very different from what we have been taught in the past. At times it may feel uncomfortable or even a bit frightening. If we have been conditioned to try to approach life entirely rationally, to follow certain rules (or to automatically rebel against them), or to do what we think other people want us to do, then beginning to follow our own inner sense of truth is a major shift. It's natural for it to take some time and it may be a little difficult and confusing at certain moments. It's important to be very compassionate with ourselves in this process.

At times we may be very aware of the conflicting voices inside of us. One part of us may be excited about making changes while another part of us is terrified about it. If we can acknowledge and honor all our different inner voices and their feelings, our intuition will show us an appropriate step to take — one that moves us in the right direction without being too frightening for our vulnerable selves or too radical for our conservative parts.

Opening New Doors

The more we practice following our intuition, the more faith we get, because we see that it really does work. Not only is nothing disastrous happening (as in our worst fears), but our lives are actually getting better and better. Remember to start with small steps until you build a sense of confidence in yourself and can gradually tackle bigger issues.

Your intuition will most likely push you

gently toward taking some appropriate risks and trying new things. For example, you might have a fantasy of doing something creative that you haven't done before, such as taking art, dancing, or music lessons. An inner critic voice might try to stop you from risking failure or embarrassment by whispering in your ear, "Don't be silly, you're not creative!" or "You're much too old to start something totally new." You can acknowledge your inner critic and thank it for its attempt to protect you from humiliation. Then you can go ahead and give it a try anyway.

Your intuition may be trying to show you that you have a new direction in which you need to move or that there is something within you that is trying to come through. If you give yourself permission to try it, you don't have to be great at it; just do it for fun. Follow your intuitive impulse and see what happens. It may open a new door for you. It may give you a chance to play and discover a new part of your personality that you haven't learned to express before.

Suppose you have always wanted to start your own business. Allow yourself to fantasize about it. Start thinking about what steps you could take in that direction. Ask your intuition to show you what to do. Try following any impulse you might have to explore this possibility. It may be that nothing will happen, or that you take a few steps and then feel blocked. This may be an indication that this is not the best course of action for you at this time. Or it may mean that you need to be open to it happening in a totally different and unexpected way. Stay open and see what happens. I know many people who have become very successful this way.

As you learn to live from your intuition you may find that the process of making decisions changes. Rather than just trying to figure things out in your head, you follow your intuitive feeling for a while and let things unfold. In the process, the right decisions usually get made.

For example, if you are unhappy in your job, don't immediately make a decision to go in and quit, unless you truly have a strong gut feeling that that is the best course of action. Instead, explore and acknowledge your feelings, such as, "I'm really unhappy here, I'd like to work with people more," or whatever. Then turn it over to your intuition and allow it to show you step by step what you need to do. You will probably find that something will emerge. You may find that your current job changes and improves, or you may get an inspiration about a different career and begin to explore that possibility. You may follow an impulse to interview for another job and find that it is right for you. Or you may get very clear that you need to resign, and it will feel appropriate to do so. The right action will emerge from the process.

If you have a problem to solve, or a desire to fulfill, try turning it over to your intuition. For example, if you feel like your social life is boring or unrewarding and you'd like to make new friends, consciously ask your intuition to guide you in this process. You might find that a week or two later you read about a hobby group and you intuitively feel drawn to attend. You may end up joining a camera club or a hiking club and find a new circle of friends with a common interest.

Some people fear that trusting their intuition will lead them to do things that are purely selfish, irresponsible, or hurtful to others. In reality, the opposite is true. Since intuition is connected to our souls and to the universal intelligence, it is always guiding us to our own highest good and the greater good for all concerned.

When we follow our intuition, we sometimes

behave in new and different ways, and others may sometimes be temporarily disappointed or upset. For example, if you are a very giving person who has always tried to please and care for others, your intuition may push you to learn to say "no" when you really don't want to do something, and to set better boundaries with people. At first, this might upset someone. In the long run, however, you and everyone else you relate to will be healthier and happier because of this change.

It's actually quite amazing to watch how the intuitive process sorts things out so that everyone ends up exactly where they need to be, doing exactly what makes them happiest.

A Guiding Force

In the process of learning to trust intuition, some people go through a period of time where they feel like their life is falling apart. Relationships may end or change dramatically, you may move, change jobs, lose interest in familiar pastimes. These are indications that you are letting go of certain aspects of your old identity. If you tried to hold onto it, you would limit or imprison yourself. The forms in your life have to change because you are changing. It's a matter of trusting that even when things are not going exactly the way you expected, there is a deeper perfection in the process. New forms of relationship, creativity, work, and home will come into being and they will reflect your growth and development.*

It's important to have emotional support while you are going through these kinds of changes. Find a friend or group of friends that you can talk to about your hopes, dreams, and fears, someone who can support and encourage you as well as give you honest feedback.

Sometimes family or old friends feel too threatened by the changes you are going through and are unable to give real support. You may need to seek out people who are interested in personal growth. One of the best ways to do this is to go to a workshop or join a support group (or create your own).

Learning to follow your intuition can sometimes feel a bit like "living on the edge." In a sense, it's learning to live without the false sense of security that comes from trying to

*For more understanding about how following your intuition can change your life, I suggest reading my book *Living in the Light*.

control everything that happens to us. It's recognizing that as we follow our inner guidance, wonderful things are going to unfold for us, things that we may not yet even imagine.

Gradually we become less afraid and more comfortable with uncertainty. We can learn to enjoy not knowing! It's actually a very exciting, alive feeling. We can learn to move into the unknown with the confidence that we have a guiding force within us that is showing us the way.

FOLLOWING YOUR OWN ENERGY MEDITATION

Sit or lie down in a comfortable position. Close your eyes. Take a deep breath and relax your body. Take another deep breath and relax your mind. Continue to breathe slowly and deeply and let go of all tension or anxiety. As you relax, you find yourself in a deep, quiet place inside. Allow yourself to just rest in that place for a few moments, with nothing you need to do or think about.

From this deep, quiet place, begin to sense the life force within you. Imagine that you are following your own energy, feeling it, trusting it, moving with it in every moment of your life. You are being completely true to yourself, speaking and living your truth. You feel alive and empowered. Imagine that you are expressing your creativity fully and freely, and let yourself enjoy the experience.

Do this meditation as often as you like. I send you my blessings on your journey.

Books

Allen, Marc. *A Visionary Life*. New World
Library, 1998.

Gawain, Shakti. *Creative Visualization*. Nataraj/
New World Library, 1978.

Gawain, Shakti. *Living in the Light*. Nataraj/
New World Library, 1986.

Gawain, Shakti. *Return to the Garden*. Nataraj/
New World Library, 1989.

Gawain, Shakti. *The Path of Transformation: How
Healing Ourselves Can Change the World*.
Nataraj/New World Library, 1993.

Gawain, Shakti. *The Four Levels of Healing: A
Guide to Balancing the Spiritual, Mental,*

Emotional, and Physical Aspects of Life.
Nataraj/New World Library, 1997.

Gawain, Shakti. *Creating True Prosperity.*
Nataraj/New World Library, 1997.

Gawain, Shakti. *Creating True Prosperity
Workbook.* Nataraj/New World Library, 1998.

Peirce, Penney. *The Intuitive Way: A Guide to
Living from Inner Wisdom.* Beyond Words
Publishing, 1997.

Roberts, Jane. *The Nature of Personal Reality.*
Amber-Allen Publishing/New World
Library, 1994.

Stone, Hal and Sidra. *Embracing Our Selves:
The Voice Dialogue Manual.* Nataraj/New
World Library, 1993.

Stone, Hal and Sidra. *Embracing Each Other:
Relationship as Teacher, Healer, and Guide.*
Nataraj/New World Library, 1993.

Stone, Sidra. *The Shadow King.* Nataraj/New
World Library, 1997.

Stone, Hal and Sidra. *Partnering.* Nataraj/New
World Library, 1999.

Vaughan, Frances E. *Awakening Intuition.*
Bantam Doubleday Dell, 1979.

Audio Tapes

Gawain, Shakti. *Living in the Light: Book on Tape*. Revised version. Nataraj/New World Library, 1998.

Gawain, Shakti. *Creative Visualization: Book on Tape*. Nataraj/New World Library, 1995.

Gawain, Shakti. *Creative Visualization Meditations*. Nataraj/New World Library, 1996.

Gawain, Shakti. *The Path of Transformation: Book on Tape*. Abridged version. Nataraj/New World Library, 1993.

Gawain, Shakti. *The Four Levels of Healing: A Guide to Balancing the Spiritual, Mental, Emotional, and Physical Aspects of Life*. Nataraj/New World Library, 1997.

Gawain, Shakti. *Creating True Prosperity: Book on Tape*. Nataraj/New World Library, 1997.

Stone, Hal and Sidra. *Meeting Your Selves*. Delos, 1990.

Stone, Hal and Sidra. *The Child Within*. Delos, 1990.

Stone, Hal and Sidra. *Meet Your Inner Critic*.

Delos, 1990.

Stone, Hal and Sidra. *Meet the Pusher*. Delos, 1990.

Stone, Hal and Sidra. *The Dance of Selves in Relationship*. Delos, 1990.

Stone, Hal and Sidra. *Understanding Your Relationships*. Delos, 1990.

Stone, Hal and Sidra. *Decoding Your Dreams*. Delos, 1990.

(All of Hal and Sidra Stone's tapes are available through Delos. See address below.)

Video Tapes

Gawain, Shakti. *The Creative Visualization Workshop Video*. Nataraj/New World Library, 1999.

Workshops

Shakti Gawain gives talks and leads workshops all over the United States and in many other countries. She also conducts retreats, intensives, and training programs. If you would like to be on her mailing list and receive workshop information, contact:

Shakti Gawain, Inc.
P.O. Box 377, Mill Valley, CA 94942
Telephone: (415) 388-7140
Fax: (415) 388-7196
E-mail: staff@shaktigawain.com
www.shaktigawain.com

For information about Drs. Hal and Sidra Stone's workshops and trainings, contact:

Delos, Inc.
P.O. Box 604, Albion, CA 95410
Telephone: (707) 937-2424
E-mail: delos@mcn.org
www.delos-inc.com

A pioneer in the field of personal growth and consciousness, Shakti Gawain is the author of many bestselling books including *Creative Visualization*, *Living in the Light*, *The Four Levels of Healing*, and *Creating True Prosperity*. She leads workshops internationally and has facilitated thousands of individuals in developing greater balance and wholeness in their lives. She and her husband live in Mill Valley, California, and on the island of Kauai.

If you enjoyed *Developing Intuition*, New World Library highly recommends the following books and cassettes:

Creative Visualization by Shakti Gawain. This pioneering bestseller and perennial favorite helped launch a new movement in the personal growth field when it was first published 20 years ago. Shakti Gawain's classic guide teaches methods that are practical and easy to incorporate into daily life.

Living in the Light: A Guide to Personal and Planetary Transformation by Shakti Gawain. In this newly updated revision of her classic bestseller, Shakti tackles the importance of listening to our intuition, relying on intuition as a guiding force in our lives, and acknowledging, working with, and embracing our disowned energies.

The Power of Now by Eckhart Tolle. Every moment is miraculous. We realize this when we stop thinking about the past and future, and find the now. This book is powerful. It can change your life instantly in the now moment.

The Seven Spiritual Laws of Success by Deepak Chopra. In *The Seven Spiritual Laws of Success*, Deepak Chopra distills the essence of his teachings into seven simple yet powerful principles that can easily be applied to create success in all areas of your life.

Signals: An Inspiring Story of Life After Life by Joel Rothschild. A profound testimony to the tenacity of the human spirit and the courage of its author. *Signals* is a work of great beauty and profound spiritual power, Everyone who has lost a loved one to death should read it.

A Visionary Life: Conversations on Personal and Planetary Evolution by Marc Allen. In this book, Marc Allen, author of *Visionary Business*, turns his attention to the vital process of building a fulfilling life. This book gives readers the simple keys to changing their lives step-by-step, helping to first envision and then move toward realizing their deepest dreams and highest aspirations.

Nataraj Publishing, a division of
New World Library, is dedicated
to publishing books and tapes that inspire
and challenge us to improve the
quality of our lives and our world.

Our books and tapes are available
in bookstores everywhere. For a catalog
of our complete library of fine books
and cassettes contact:

Nataraj Publishing/New World Library
14 Pamaron Way
Novato, CA 94949
Tel: (415) 884-2100
Fax: (415) 884-2199
Or call toll-free: (800) 972-6657
Catalog requests: Ext. 50
Ordering: Ext. 52
E-mail: escort@nwlib.com
www.newworldlibrary.com